# TOTALLY BOGUS (BUT TRUE) TALES FROM THE 1980S

**WILL PADILLA**

Copyright © 2025 by Will Padilla

No part of this publication may be reproduced, distributed, or transmitted in any form or by any means, including photocopying, recording, or other electronic or mechanical methods, without the prior written permission of the publisher, except as permitted by U.S. copyright law.

ISBN 979-8-218-67469-4

1980snow.com

## CONTENT ADVISORY

The stories within this book were chosen because of the popularity of true crime. That said, the following tales are not of the grisly variety typical of that genre. Be warned, however, that some do include mature topics. "The Monster with 21 Faces" references suicide. "The Real Story of Cocaine Bear" unsurprisingly discusses the illicit substance. That story and "The Montauk Project" also refer to murder. These references, however, are tangential to the main tale, and the authors attempt to present them tactfully.

To Kat and Jon in the backseat,
one more word and I'll turn this thing around

Strange things are afoot at the Circle K.
—Ted "Theodore" Logan, *Bill & Ted's Excellent Adventure*

Live people ignore the strange and unusual.
I myself am strange and unusual.
—Lydia Deetz, *Beetlejuice*

You're weird. Thank God, you're weird.
—Elizabeth Solley, *The Fog*

# TOTALLY BOGUS (BUT TRUE) TALES FROM THE 1980S

# CONTENTS

- **i** Preface
- **1** Strangest Things: The Montauk Project
- **9** The Adventure for Swordquest
- **19** The Most Artful Museum Heist
- **25** The Real Cocaine Bear
- **33** 1999: The Accidental Prophecy
- **43** The Rendlesham Incident
- **53** Rapper's Delight: These Are the Good Crimes
- **65** The Monster with 21 Faces
- **75** The Cabbage Patch Paternity Suit
- **83** Masquerade
- **93** Game Over for Atari "Champ"
- **99** The Mystery of the Garfield Phone
- **105** About the Author
- **109** Acknowledgements
- **111** Sources

## PREFACE

In the 1980s, long before everyone had a WOPR in their pocket, weird things happened. And like the fashion of the decade, those events were colorful. Without the convenience of modern technology, however, many of the most fascinating tales weren't as widely known. After all, only so many stories could be told on *That's Incredible*. Only so many yarns could be spun on the pages of *Ripley's Believe It or Not!* This book is my humble contribution to the media that kept my generation curious and occasionally frightened. It's a collection of those strange-but-true moments—real stories from the decade of big hair and even bigger mysteries.

The tales that follow were first told on my podcast *1980s Now*. It's a weekly show that celebrates the pop culture moments that define that decade and continue to influence contemporary media. As true crime podcasts gained popularity, those programs reminded me of my own youthful hunger for unsolved mysteries. While my interests included criminal activities, I also yearned to learn more about the uncanny events that left us questioning our world.

Gratefully, many outlets in the 1970s and 1980s shared those stranger-than-fiction tales. On television, I devoured episodes of *In*

*Search Of…* and *Arthur C. Clarke's Mysterious World* and the revival of *Ripley's Believe It or Not!* Once we had a VCR at home, I rented films purporting to be based on true stories, like *The Amityville Horror*, *The Philadelphia Experiment* and the documentary *The Man Who Saw Tomorrow*. And when I had consumed all of those, I grabbed a fist full of coins and rode the bus to the library. There, I'd pore over Time-Life's *The Enchanted World* and later *Mysteries of the Unknown* ("Read the book!"). Whether I was learning about serial killers or cryptids, I was mesmerized, sometimes terrified, and loved every moment of it.

While many of the tales told to us in our youths were from previous generations, my 1980s podcast had me longing to share stories from our favorite decade. As with other media of that era, many of the curious tales from the 1980s are not only fascinating, but they've had a larger impact on society since. So, *1980s Now* began sharing the bizarre, and often forgotten, yarns from the decade of our youths. And as listeners kept asking for more of these jaw-dropping tales, it became obvious: these stories needed a home in print. And I was eager to have them join the legacy of books and other media that fueled my fascination for the bizarre when I was young.

To tell these often complicated stories in an entertaining, and easily digestible way, we often had to simplify some of their details. In some instances, a single, seemingly accurate account of these tales was not available. Instead, only conflicting versions could be found. When that occurred, we chose the most fascinating of the varying facts, while endeavoring to tell an accurate story.

On the other hand, some of these strange tales required that we make them more layered. To tell a more complete tale, we found ourselves including details that had us weave together interrelated plots, occasionally from different time periods.

As a result of our efforts, we believe what follows are the best versions of these stories. They're unusual and engaging and presented in a manner that will have you retelling them to others. If you're hungry for more details, however, please see the "Sources" section at the end of the book. (And if you'd like to hear my co-hosts' often ridiculous takes on these tales, check out those episodes of *1980s Now* by visiting 1980snow.com.)

Finally, I hope the above highlights the challenge of documenting the quirky stories contained here. Researching and consuming, and then condensing and writing, these tales is demanding. Doing that while attempting to entertain is even more difficult. So, I'm lucky to have two friends who are not only as fascinated by pop culture as I am, but are also excellent storytellers. "The Adventure for Swordquest" and "Masquerade" were written by talented screenwriter George W. Krubski. "1999: The Accidental Prophecy" was written by music expert Marcus Taylor. In addition to their efforts here, they've also been regular contributors to the *1980s Now* podcast, upon which—as I mentioned earlier—these stories were first shared.

Inside these pages, you'll find accounts of criminal oddities, alleged supernatural encounters, and unusual pop culture phenomena—events so peculiar they read like fiction. And while the title of this book invokes slang popularized by Bill S. Preston, Esq. and Ted "Theodore" Logan, every one of them is real. Or, at least, "real." For even the unbelievable stories—those that would serve as plots for movies and TV shows (and do)—are maintained as fact by those who allegedly experienced them.

And while some made headlines, and others went the way of the waterbed, all of them speak to a truth that's unsettling and entertaining. The 1980s weren't just weird. They were like totally weird for reals to the max. Word! So, turn the page and prepare to be surprised. The truth isn't just out there—it's got a Walkman, a mullet, and one hell of a story to tell.

# STRANGEST THINGS:
# THE MONTAUK PROJECT

Although it was late 1955, the anonymous package read "Happy Easter" when it arrived at the U.S. Office of Naval Research (ONR). Once opened, it revealed a copy of Morris K. Jessup's book *The Case for the UFO: Unidentified Flying Objects*. This curious edition, however, was filled with handwritten notes in different shades of ink, appearing to capture a debate between three individuals. The trio, it seemed, agreed upon two things: (1) The author of the book was close to discovering their secret; and (2) something must be done.

A year after the ONR received the unusual publication, they summoned the author to explain the annotated book. Immediately upon examination, Jessup noticed something familiar. The handwriting of the scribbled notes resembled that on a series of letters he had received from Carl Allen. In those correspondences, Allen told tale of secret government research that used the unpublished theories of Albert Einstein. Allen claimed that in 1943, an experiment to make the U.S.S. Eldridge invisible to radar instead vanished the Navy ship from existence before it reappeared in the Philadelphia shipyard minutes later. And when it returned, the vessel was the stuff of nightmares. Some of the sailors were fused with the ship, their bodies intertwined with the steel. Those more fortunate simply went mad.

Long Island, NY, 1971. Electrical engineer Preston Nichols did not believe in paranormal activity. So, he was thrilled to receive a grant to disprove the existence of mental telepathy. To his surprise, however, Nichols soon determined that psychic phenomena not only existed, but it behaved much like the radio frequencies with which he was more familiar. And in 1974, a few years into his research, Nichols noticed something peculiar about the psychics he had been studying. Every day, at the same hour, their abilities would be rendered ineffective. Their thoughts were "jammed."

Suspecting that the psychic interference was caused by an electronic signal, Nichols scanned the airwaves. Soon, he learned that whenever the telepaths were rendered powerless, a 410-420 megahertz frequency appeared. But from where? Desperate to find the source, Nichols placed a modified TV antenna atop the roof of his car, attached it to a VHF receiver, and went driving. The powerful signal made quick of Nichols' task, leading him straight to the eastern tip of Long Island. The frequency was coming directly from a football field-sized radar reflector sitting precariously atop a building on the Montauk Air Force base

Long before the Montauk Air Force based was established, the eastern tip of Long Island held strategic significance. Nearly 200 years before Nichols went snooping, the Montauk Lighthouse was authorized to keep watch for British ships during the American Revolution. And because its location midway between two major American cities made it vulnerable to invasion, the military installation continued to grow throughout the first and second World Wars. To protect it from German spies in the 1940s, the base was even fashioned to look like a typical New England fishing village. But what was it hiding in 1974?

When Nichols found the source of the telepathic Kryptonite, he thought it must have been generated accidentally. Although the base was still active in 1974, Nichols couldn't imagine a use for an antiquated radar system. Unfortunately, the tight-lipped security stationed there were of no help to Nichols. They would only say that the array was used as part of an FAA project. And while Nichols found this justification to be unbelievable, it was not as remarkable as the truth Nichols would later discover. But he would need to wait a decade before he would remember it.

It was 1984. Nichols had been researching metaphysical phenomena for thirteen years, when he learned the Montauk Airforce Base had been shuttered. Finally, Nichols could examine the mysterious installation without fear. Or so he thought. When Nichols returned to the now abandoned base, he found the main gate was open, and the windows and doors of the buildings throughout were likewise left ajar. Furniture, equipment and documents were everywhere. It was as if the military base had been deserted, and in haste.

As Nichols searched through the debris-strewn Airforce station, he found the remains of odd high voltage equipment. But his most curious discovery was a man living among it. When the stranger's eyes fell upon Nichols, however, he was more frightened than Nichols. "It's you," the man said, sounding terrified. He then explained that he had not only been living at the deserted base, but he had been working there when it was abandoned a year earlier. The stranger told Nichols that an experiment had forced the military to flee. The secret project had opened a portal to hell and freed one of its monsters, he explained. And the man who led this endeavor, the stranger concluded, was Nichols.

Nichols doubted the unusual man's story. After all, Nichols had never worked at the Montauk Airforce Base. And monsters from hell were the stuff of B-movies. Nevertheless, Nichols continued to research the mysteries of Montauk. As he spoke to long-term residents of the community, their bizarre accounts only raised more questions. Several townsfolk told Nichols it once snowed in August. The Chief of Police revealed that crimes were perpetrated in specific two hour blocks. And many recalled animals overrunning the town en masse. As the puzzles mounted, a man appeared at Nichol's lab bringing with him potential solutions and the threat of murder.

When Duncan Cameron arrived at Nichols' doorstep, he seemed too eager to help. Immediately suspicious, Nichols did what he had done with anything else out of the norm. He sought to connect Cameron to Montauk. So, Nichols drove Cameron to the Air Force Base, and to his surprise, Cameron not only recognized it, but he knew many of its minute details. But before Nichols could learn how Cameron had gained such familiarity, something even stranger occurred. When the pair entered the transmitter room, Cameron fell into a trance. With his eyes vacant, Cameron began spewing information uncontrollably. The most shocking of his revelations: he had been programmed to befriend Nichols, destroy his lab, and kill him.

Cameron was as shocked as Nichols to learn of his deadly programming. Now free of it, however, Cameron committed himself to helping Nichols unravel the mysteries of Montauk. As luck would have it, the pair soon realized that Cameron was "an extremely operational psychic." And as Cameron began recalling more memories that had been hidden from him, so too did Nichols begin to remember long-dormant experiences. While there was still much to be learned about what he began calling "The Montauk Project," Nichols was now certain he had been involved. But it wasn't until six years later, that Nichols would learn just how.

By 1990, Nichols had spent six years attempting to uncover the truth about Montauk. He had stumbled upon a high-level secret project, and feared it may cost him his life. So, he went public. Nichols gave an unannounced lecture at the United States Psychotronics Association. Next, he shared military documents he discovered at the abandoned base with an unnamed U.S. Senator. Perhaps safer, Nichols still didn't know his own seeming role in the project. That is, until he constructed a Delta-T antenna on the roof of his laboratory. As he soldered the wires together, connections in his subconscious were also made. Suddenly, Nichols remembered everything.

Nichols learned he began working for the Montauk Project in the early 1970s. The extra-governmental organization had been formed to continue the controversial scientific goals of predecessors from decades earlier. The team was to create metaphysical tools that could assist the U.S. military. To assist their paranormal goals, the project made use of the so-called Montauk Chair. First constructed in the 1950s, the chair leveraged the abilities of the psychic sitting upon it, amplifying their powers. In the 1970s, while Nichols worked on the project, that role fell to Cameron. And while the technology that powered the unusual furniture wasn't fully understood, it was believed much of it was provided by the Sirians, a race of aliens who hail from the star system known as Sirius.

Over a decade later, the project had not only made significant progress, but their research also yielded metaphysical phenomena beyond their dreams—and nightmares. While mind control finally seemed attainable, they also learned the Montauk Chair could manifest objects from Cameron's thoughts. And further experimenting with this form of conjuring led the team to discover time travel. With the proper attuning, the chair allowed Cameron to open portals to other eras. And while these discoveries were exciting, when Nichols and Cameron learned the project's true goal, they feared the worst. The researchers were attempting to open a time door to the U.S.S. Eldridge in 1943.

By 1983, Nichols' and Cameron's concerns piqued. The project, they determined, must be stopped. To do so, they would leverage the combined powers of the Montauk Chair and Cameron's psychic abilities. But they weren't quite sure when they would enact this contingency. That is, until August 12. On that day, Nichols and Cameron continued their experiments as ordered, when strange phenomena suddenly began. The otherworldly equipment started to whir and click until it appeared to synch with something beyond the scientists' perception. Then, a time portal opened. On the other side, the U.S.S. Eldridge appeared. It was time to destroy the project.

As the others gathered at the Montauk Airforce Base stared into the temporal doorway in amazement, Nichols crept to Cameron (who was still in the Montauk Chair) and whispered, "The time is now." Immediately, Cameron imagined a hideous monster, and nearly instantaneously, the Montauk Chair conjured the beast before him. The horrifying creature began feasting on anyone in its sights, destroying everything that stood between it and its prey. The surviving commanders ordered Nichols to shut down the generators powering the equipment. But that failed to stop the beast. The experiment continued unabated as if powered by another force. So, Nichols destroyed the equipment itself. And finally, the monster faded into the ether.

Following the events of August 12, 1983, the Montauk Air Force Station was abandoned. The most important, and incriminating, equipment was removed. And, according to the legend, those who survived the deadly incident had their memories wiped.

Today, it's possible to visit Camp Hero, the home of the base, which opened to the public as a state park in 2002. You may not want to linger too long, however. Because according to some, the experiments continue in secret today.

# THE ADVENTURE FOR SWORDQUEST
## by George W. Krubski

Our tale begins with a humble gray dot. The year: 1980. The age of Atari was upon us. A million units were sold and a dozen and a half games released. One was *Adventure*. Conceived as a graphic version of text games like *Zork*, it's now hailed as one of the most influential video games of all time. *Adventure* was the first action-adventure and console fantasy game. In 1980, it was enough that it delivered on the promise of its name, sending players on a quest to recover an enchanted treasure stolen by an evil magician. But slaying dragons, finding hidden keys, and recovering the goblet were just the beginning. For concealed deep within *Adventure* was a second, stranger quest, one unknown to the adventurer.

In August of 1980, a youth from Salt Lake City sent a handwritten letter to Atari, claiming he had "found something strange" while exploring the catacombs within the game's Black Castle. He detailed how he discovered a tiny, hidden speck, and how he used this Gray Dot to enter a mysterious, otherwise inaccessible room elsewhere in the game. There, the boy discovered the final treasure: a secret. The hidden room revealed a mystery that had been withheld from the world with one simple message: "Created by Warren Robinett."

Warren Robinett, the architect of *Adventure*, was no longer with Atari by the time of the game's release. So, he was certain the company would be angered by his act of rebellion, and strip his secret credit from future releases of *Adventure*. He was wrong. Instead, the unusual tale of the Gray Dot became the first and best-known Easter Egg in all of video game lore. With *Adventure* a success, fueled by the intrigue of the Gray Dot, Atari looked to spawn a successor. But before long, their next evolution in gaming would grow into something wholly new, uniquely ambitious, and difficult to tame.

Atari's new "Adventure Series" was advertised as early as 1981, with two games promised for the following year. One article hailed *Swordquest* as the most promising of Atari's forthcoming products, calling it "a four-part epic mystery that, believe it or not, may take a full year to unravel." The *Swordquest* saga would follow twins Tarra and Torr on a sprawling journey for the Sword of Ultimate Sorcery, bringing them into conflict with their parents' murderer, the evil King Tyrannus. Each chapter would lead into the next, but could also be played as a standalone adventure. Nothing like it had been attempted before. And for good reason. For the scope of the ambitious story was only the beginning of Atari's audacity.

To win each game, players would unearth clues concealed not only within the confines of their TV screens, but also in a companion comic book that accompanied each cartridge. Since Atari's parent company

Warner Communications also owned DC Comics, they recruited comic book royalty to tell the tale of this epic quest. Roy Thomas (best known for introducing Conan the Barbarian to a generation of comic book readers) and Gerry Conway (who drafted the gut-wrenching death of Gwen Stacy) were brought in to write. Art was provided by George Perez (who was working on DC's bestselling *New Teen Titans* at the time) and Dick Giordano (whose pedigree extended back to Charlton Comics). But more was to come. A treasure hunt as daring as *Swordquest* demanded an equally compelling prize, and Atari planned to exceed all expectations.

The Talisman of Penultimate Truth. The Chalice of Light. The Crown of Life. The Philosopher's Stone. To their great fortune—or misadventure—Warner Bros. also owned the Franklin Mint. While these sounded like mere in-game treasures, Warner was uniquely positioned to bring these artifacts to dazzling life. And so, they did. Each chapter of *Swordquest* was to culminate in a contest allowing a clever hero to claim one of these real-life treasures, each valued at $25,000. But wait, there was more. The four paragons who conquered each chapter were to face one another in a final challenge to claim the Sword of Ultimate Sorcery, a jewel-encrusted blade worth $50,000. A treasure hunt like no other, you say? A quest for the ages, yes! But a tale, perhaps, too good to be true.

*Earthworld*, the first of the planned four-part adventure series, arrived in October 1982 with promises of zodiac-themed adventures pitting players against challenges like the Dark Bull Pit of Taurus and the deadly Spears of Sagittarius. But those dreaming of a thrilling game that would up the stakes from *Adventure* would have to wait another month for the *Raiders of the Lost Ark* video game. Instead, *Earthworld's* challengers were met with an intellectual puzzle spread across a dozen bland rooms. True, some included reflex-related mini-games, but mostly, players found "magical objects," carried them to different rooms, and hoped some combination of the artifacts would reveal a clue in the form of a pair of numbers. But what to do with those mysterious numbers?

Soon, the most adept players discovered that each set of numbers mapped to a page and panel in the game's corresponding comic book, which held an artfully concealed word. Five of these words formed the game winning phrase "QUEST IN TOWER, TALISMAN FOUND." And with twelve rooms, sixteen objects—and an untold number of complex combinations of those—it's amazing that anyone successfully completed the game, which one honest Atari employee referred to as "the kind of a punishment a judge might mete out to a convicted serial killer." Yet, in the months that followed, thousands of hopeful heroes embraced the torture and deciphered the code. And eventually, eight Supreme Sages of Sorcery—the titled granted to those correctly identifying the phrase—appeared, ready to battle one another.

In May of 1983, the champions of *Earthworld* gathered at Atari headquarters for a contest that was equal parts *Willy Wonka* and *The Last*

*Starfighter*. A diverse group, including high school and college students, a housewife, and a Coast Guard lieutenant, raced to best a modified version of *Earthworld*. Their bounty: the Talisman of Penultimate Truth, an 18-karat solid gold disc studded with twelve diamonds, the birthstones of the twelve Zodiac signs, and a miniature white gold sword set atop it. Ultimately, in a mere 47 minutes, 27-year-old Stephen Bell emerged victorious, attributing his win to his knowledge of astrology and his ability to decipher the unique clues provided. And although Bell claimed he was excited to show his prize to his parents, he also spoke of selling the medallion to buy a car.

By the time the *Earthworld* competition took place, *Fireworld* had been out for three months. Having learned some lessons, Atari reduced the number of rooms to ten, provided better clues, and made the pattern of objects less confoundingly random. Consequently, 73 Knights of the Chalice identified the correct phrase "LEADS TO CHALICE, POWER ABOUNDS." To narrow the field to 50 contestants, Atari employed an essay. The competition was set for November, but in an early sign of the troubles to come, it was postponed until January 1984. In the end, Michael Rideout claimed the Chalice of Light, setting up a battle of the ages against *Earthworld's* champion, Stephen Bell. But alas, it was a battle that would never come to pass. For evil forces outside the realm of *Swordquest* had been gathering in number.

A year earlier in 1982, Atari released three games crafted by brilliant designer Howard Scott Warshaw. Like the *Swordquest* series, Warshaw's works were influenced by Warren Robinett's Gray Dot. Unlike *Swordquest*, however, Warshaw kept his Easter Eggs buried. May 1982 brought Warshaw's *Yar's Revenge*, the first game to come with its own comic. November saw the arrival of *Raiders of the Lost Ark*, the true spiritual successor to *Adventure* that *Earthworld* strived to be. And as the year ended, so too did the Warshaw trilogy, as the eagerly anticipated *E.T. the Extra-Terrestrial* filled store shelves. Unfortunately, however, to meet the demands of the Christmas season, development time, which was often ten months or more, was cut to mere weeks, leading to events that would impact not only *Swordquest*, but the entire industry.

In the years following, it became clear that numerous factors were responsible for the collapse of the video game industry in 1983: a glut of game systems, the rise of home computers, and the unchecked quality of third-party competitors. But the character who was so beloved on theater screens a year earlier, had become a pariah on our game console. *E.T.* was considered such a singularly disappointing game that it became the face of the fall. And so, it came to be that in September 1983, while warriors fought feverishly to uncover the treasures of *Fireworld*, Atari sent truckloads of unsellable cartridges to be buried in the New Mexico desert.

The video game industry had imploded. Although the impact would not be felt immediately, a new King would usurp the throne at Atari. Jack Tramiel, one of the world's leading "business-as-war-entrepreneurs," ruled Atari ruthlessly, cutting staff by 90% and earning comparisons to *Star Wars* villain Darth Vader. Tramiel's strategy for the failing brand was lean and hungry, unsentimental, and driven by sales. It left little room for flights of fancy. Or for quests for fantasy. And so, Atari dispatched the envoys feared most throughout the land, the very Destroyers of Dreams: attorneys.

In another foreboding omen, the third game, *Waterworld*, was available only to Atari Club members. To further dumb it down, it featured only eight rooms, a hint book, and a mere four-word solution ("HASTEN TOWARD REVEALED CROWN.") But those that survived the aquatic challenges in search of the Crown of Life were told that the contest was delayed until late 1984. That is until it was delayed until 1985. Then, potential warriors were once again asked to submit essays to narrow down the challengers to ten or fifteen—numbers vary according to the lore—but then were told they didn't make the cut. By 1986, it was clear, the third contest would never take place. *Swordquest*, the most bizarre and ambitious treasure hunt in the history of video games, was over. Or was it?

Although there was no public competition for *Waterworld's* Crown of Life, folklore tells of a contest held in secret. In response to a query in 1984 questioning if the entire *Swordquest* series was a "phony come-on," *Electronic Fun with Computers & Games* magazine stated that the first three contests had taken place. Until his untimely death in 2020, gaming historian Curt Vendel was adamant that Atari had held the match, and that the Crown of Life had been claimed by a mysterious champion.

The final chapter, *Airworld*, however, died on the vine. Despite tales that the game was playable, Tod Frye, who worked on all four games, said it was only 20% complete before being unceremoniously terminated. And while others claim to have seen a script or storyboard for the comic, artist George Perez dismissed this as nonsense. By the mid-1980s, *Swordquest* was truly dead. But nothing stays buried forever.

Even stronger than four elements of *Swordquest* is nostalgia. In 2014, more than 30 years after the video game crash, the mysteries of the treasure buried in the New Mexico desert were unearthed, revealing a trove of *E.T.*, and other video game cartridges. Among others, the dig was attended by Howard Scott Warshaw. Well publicized, including a documentary, it helped draw attention to later chapters of the Atari saga. And so it came to be that three years later, Dynamic Comics released a new *Swordquest* comic book, telling the tale of an adult gamer trying to track down and play *Airworld* to complete his childhood quest. And last year, Atari 50, a compilation of over 100 video games, and a documentary of the history of Atari, finally completed the *Swordquest* saga by releasing *Airworld*. Players may at long last claim the Sword of Ultimate Sorcery…in game, at least. But what about the treasures in the real world, those forged by the Franklin Mint?

*Fireworld* champion, Michael Rideout, is still in possession of the Chalice of Light, which he secured in a safe deposit box. But according to both Rideout and historian Curt Vendel, while Stephen Bell may have kept the gems and a small sword emblem that hung from the Talisman of

Penultimate Truth, he melted down the medallion and sold the precious metals. No one has ever come forward as owner of the Crown of Life, but if the *Waterworld* contest was held, someone has it. Conventional wisdom dictates that the final treasure, the Sword of Ultimate Sorcery, which was valued at $50,000, was returned to the Franklin Mint to be melted down and likely repurposed as dozens of commemorative coins. But eagle-eyed employees noticed that Jack Tramiel had a unique-looking sword hanging in his office. And while some claimed it was a family heirloom, we may never know for certain. And thus, our tale ends as it began, mired in mystery. Or does it?

Although a version of *Airworld* was eventually released, the solution does not include a phrase. The *Swordquest* quatrain, begun over 40 years ago, remains incomplete. "QUEST IN TOWER, TALISMAN FOUND / LEADS TO CHALICE, POWER ABOUNDS / HASTEN TOWARD REVEALED CROWN…" The first three games tracked a series of clues from video game to comic. So, is it just coincidence that recent years have given us a new video game and a new comic? Perhaps the clues are still out there to lead a new champion to the Sword of Ultimate Sorcery (or Jack Tramiel's office). Perhaps the true *Swordquest* is just waiting for brave soul to accept the challenge. Will you take up the adventure?

## THE MOST ARTFUL MUSEUM HEIST

Mexico, December 1985. Before that particular Christmas, Carlos Perches Treviño and Ramón Sardina García, both in their twenties, were considered quite boring. Belonging to middle-class families, the pair was studying veterinary medicine at the Universidad Nacional Autónoma de México. In addition to their interest in animals, both Perches and Sardina shared a fascination with pre-Hispanic art. And perhaps because it was much more interesting than taking a dog's temperature, their shared passion led to a collective obsession with the National Museum of Anthropology. That locale was central to both the conservation of Mexican heritage and the young men's get-rich-quick crime.

At 1 am, just an hour after Christmas Eve slipped into Christmas, Perches and Sardina slipped behind the National Museum in search of a secret passage into the building. Their moves, however, did not rely on luck. The soon-to-be thieves had spent the prior six months casing the joint. While other veterinary students may have enjoyed their summer respite, this pair spent more than 50 visits learning the daily routines of the museum's security guards. They examined display cases, took photographs, and studied construction layouts. Their efforts identified key vulnerabilities in the institution's defenses. Early Christmas morning, they had determined was the best time for their plan. And the air conditioning duct was the most discrete way to execute it.

While visions of sugar plums *bailaban en las cabezas de* the security guards, Perches and Sardina *Die Hard*-ed their way into the building. By belly crawling through the air ducts, the pair eluded security cameras and the alarm system, and soon breached the museum. Arriving in the gallery, the criminals found not a creature was stirring, not even an underpaid security guard. Their surveillance had paid off. As anticipated, the museum's personnel—who were charged with patrolling the 161,000 square feet of the 26-room building every two hours—were gathered in one room, celebrating the holiday.

As security presumably exchanged white elephant gifts of Care Bears and Transformers, Perches and Sardina quietly made their way to the galleries featuring the artifacts of the Maya, Mixteca and Mexica civilizations. Ignoring dozens of display cases, the thieves focused on the most valuable exhibits. Their targets, the pieces that were worth the most per square inch, were placed inside a suitcase. And after toiling away for an undisturbed three hours, the pair slunk away as surreptitiously as they arrived. Once outside the museum, the two robbers fled in their waiting Volkswagen and disappeared.

While the Three Kings hadn't yet delivered gifts to Mexican children, the morning shift at the National Museum of Anthropology learned that two jokers had robbed them. The museum reported 124 precious objects had been stolen. Those included objects from the sacred cenote of Chichén Itzá, more than 60 Mayan pieces from the Temple of Palenque, gold jewelry from the Mixteca, and the famous mask of the Zapotec Bat God. The treasures were made of gold, jade, turquoise, and obsidian. The value of just one of the pieces exceeded $20 million at the time (about $58.5 million today). The damage to Mexico's culture, however, was priceless. Museum curator Felipe Solís lamented, "What they've stolen from us is a piece of our history… [something] of inestimable anthropological and historical value."

The scandal became worldwide news. The response was quick. The value and cultural significance of the stolen artifacts led authorities to suspect the work of international thieves. So, in addition to the cooperation of the immigration body, personnel from the General Directorate of Customs, workers from the country's airports and Interpol, more than 30 people were tasked with solving the case. And while police plastered Mexico with wanted posters at docks, airports, and railroad stations, Interpol kept an ear out for black market sales of archeological items. But for the next four years, not a single clue could be found.

Immediately after the heist, the hopeful-veterinarians-turned-cat-burglars first fled to Perches' parents' home in the suburbs on the outskirts of Mexico City. The suitcase filled with the priceless artifacts was hidden on the top shelf of the closet in Perches' room. With the world looking for them, the pair decided to lay low. But in actuality, the duo had no plans of selling their ill-gotten loot. That changed, however, after Perches moved to Acapulco. Upon taking refuge there, Perches established ties with drug traffickers, who offered to help sell the pieces on the black market. But it would be Perches who would be sold out.

In January 1989, police arrested drug trafficker Salvador Gutiérrez, who was also known as El Cabo. Gutiérrez offered authorities information he hoped would reduce his sentence. He told tale of the enterprising burglar he had met in Acapulco—and shared the whereabouts of the stolen museum pieces. With the location of the invaluable items known, all that remained was to capture the elusive thieves. That required some subterfuge by authorities. The deputy prosecutor in Mexico's "War on Drugs" placed wiretaps in prisons and monitored all calls between Gutiérrez and Perches. Soon, their work was rewarded. In one not-so-private conversation, Perches negotiated the sale of gems from what he described as "the greatest art [collection] in Mexico." This would prove enough to capture him.

Just six months after Carlos Perches Treviño had been identified as the most brazen thief in Mexican history, police raided a home in the suburb of Jardines de San Mateo. There, authorities recovered 111 of the 124 stolen pieces. They were found in a duffel bag, wrapped in toilet paper, still in the closet of Perches' room at his parents' house. Of the missing pieces, Perches had exchanged two for cocaine, seven had remained with Perches' cohort Ramón Sardina García, and the whereabouts of four others was unknown. Regardless of the initial difficulties they faced, the authorities managed to recover practically all of the most valuable pieces, including the mask of the Zapotec Bat God.

During his interrogation, Perches admitted to being the mastermind behind the robbery. Among the details the loquacious criminal provided to investigators, however, Perches didn't explain why he and his accomplice Sardina had committed the crime of the century. He was also unable to provide the location of Sardina, who remains at large today. It's believed that the seven pieces Sardina controlled never left Mexico. Likewise, Perches never left the country. Having been sentenced to 22 years in prison, he was released early in 1995. Shortly thereafter, he was murdered under mysterious circumstances.

## THE REAL COCAINE BEAR

It was in November 1985. While trudging through the fallen leaves of the Chattahoochee National Forest, a hunter came upon easy prey. Lying there before him, in a small clearing beneath a canopy of trees, was a sizeable black bear. Though it was as still as death, it appeared alive. And so, the hunter, slowly raised his rifle, bringing the butt of the gun tight against his shoulder. But before he could squeeze the trigger, he made another, more startling discovery. Strewn about the body of the *Ursus americanus*, were several packages of a white substance. And nearby, was a large duffle bag. The bear was already dead, killed by man who had left a string of deaths long before this Yogi had dined on the deadly pic-a-nic basket.

With a name that sounds like the villain from a 1980s movie, Andrew Carter Thornton IIII was born into Kentucky's blue-blood society. A child of privilege, Thornton forewent his family's esteemed horse farm for a seeming life of public service. After graduating from the prestigious Sewanee Military Academy in 1962, Thornton joined the U.S. Army. There, Thornton became a decorated paratrooper for the 82nd

Airborne Division. Despite his extensive training, Thornton wasn't prepared for the jump that would end his life.

Longing to continue the adrenaline-fueled combat he had experienced, Thornton joined the Lexington-Fayette Urban County Police Department in 1968, just a few years after his military career had ended. And as police work became routine, Thornton's thrill-seeking ambition landed him on the newly formed narcotics squad. Working closely with the DEA, Thornton's need-for-speed was sated, albeit briefly, as he raced off to stop one drug bust after another. But soon, confiscating drugs wasn't nearly as exciting as selling them.

Lifelong friends, Bradley Bryant traveled in the same high-class social circles as Thornton. The pair even attended the Military Academy together. So, in 1977, when Bryant formed a private security company, it was only natural for Bryant to court Thornton away from the police department. Thornton turned in his badge that year and joined Bryant in the new venture. Jimmy Chargra, one of their first clients, however, seemed to need little protection. When this leader of a large drug-running syndicate was scheduled to appear before a U.S. District Judge he couldn't bribe, he had him murdered. The hitman: Charles Harrelson, father of beloved *Cheers* actor Woody.

In September 1979, the China Lake Naval Weapons Center, an installation that conducts highly classified research in the barren reaches of the Mojave Desert, had been robbed. Sophisticated and deadly military equipment, including infrared nightscopes, had been stolen.

Already fearing the extensive illegal exporting of arms from the United States, federal authorities were on high alert.

On January 4, 1980, while the disappearance of the equipment was under investigation on the West Coast, the Philadelphia police responded to what they believed was a routine call. A maid at an airport hotel had smelled marijuana emanating from one particular room. Once inside, however, drugs were the least interesting item the officers uncovered.

While some may pack pajamas, clean underwear, and a toothbrush, while traveling, Bradley Bryant was prepared for something else when police arrested him. In addition to his skivvies, Bryant was carrying a cache of semi-automatic weapons, an assortment of disguises, more than ten fraudulent Kentucky driver's licenses, and $22,000 in cash.

When Bryant's arrest led to the additional search of a warehouse he rented in Lexington, officers found an arsenal of weapons, various electronic surveillance devices, and an apparently stolen infrared nightscope. Also among Bryant's items was a notebook that contained the names and addresses of two dozen men, including one Lexington resident: Andrew Carter Thornton III.

Within days of Bryant's arrest, several federal agencies joined the investigation. And just a few months later, 25 individuals were indicted in Fresno, California, charged with conspiracy to import and distribute marijuana, and to steal government property from the China Lake Naval Base Weapons Center. Although Thornton was named in that indictment, he was not charged. Instead, amid hints of a larger drug-smuggling conspiracy, Thornton was arrested for piloting a DC4 loaded with a literal half ton of ganja. Sensing justice was coming for him, Thornton fled.

A "prepper," Thornton had been practicing for the apocalypse for years. Now, with his world coming to an end, Thornton donned a bulletproof vest, carried a pistol, and eluded capture for several months. But when U.S. Customs discovered the 56-foot converted mine sweeper that they had seized off the coast of Louisiana carried 1,500 pounds of marijuana—and a machine gun belonging to Thornton—the search intensified. After Thornton was finally apprehended, U.S. marshals transported him to Fresno for his arraignment, where he posted $75,000 in cash and a $1 million personal surety bond, secured by possibly the only remaining connection Thornton had to his prior life as a Kentucky aristocrat: three racehorses.

On February 27, 1982, just three days before Thornton was scheduled to appear for a hearing in Fresno, it appeared vigilante justice was served. As he left a restaurant, Thornton was shot twice in the chest at close range. But the .38-caliber "wadcutter" bullets didn't penetrate the bulletproof vest Thornton wore as often as others wear socks. But it wasn't good fortune that kept Thornton alive, because the police quickly determined the mastermind behind the apparent attempted murder: it was Thornton himself. The attack had been staged by Thornton to persuade the judge that his life would be endangered should he be incarcerated.

Ultimately, Thornton pleaded no contest to marijuana conspiracy charges. And while Bryant had already begun serving a fifteen-year sentence, Thornton received what was effectively a slap on the wrist: six months at a minimum-security facility and a $500 fine. But the convictions of his co-conspirators did more damage to Thornton than jail time. Already quite paranoid, Thornton shrunk his circle of trust to himself and his karate instructor turned bodyguard, Bill Leonard. Following his release from prison, Thornton divorced himself from the crime ring he had helped to create and decided to resume his drug smuggling operations alone. But there was still a matter of some loose ends that needed to be tightened.

For three years, authorities sought Thornton for questioning regarding what they described as "vendetta deaths." A series of otherwise unrelated murder victims were connected by Thornton's enterprises. Gene Berry, the Florida state's attorney, who had successfully prosecuted one of Thornton's co-defendants, was murdered at point blank range when he opened the door to his Punta Gorda residence. Robert S. Walker, a witness against Thornton in the case, was found strangled in a swamp in Tampa. The man who informed Customs of Thornton's involvement with the Louisiana smuggling vessel had his throat slit in Miami.

On September 9, 1985, Thornton began what would be his final, fateful journey. Having invited Leonard to vacation with him in the Bahamas, the pair boarded a Cessna 404. An accomplished pilot, Thornton steered the craft through the darkness, and the rain, and flew completely over the Bahamas. It was then that Thornton revealed the true nature of the trip. Instead of snorkeling on the Caribbean island, Leonard was to help Thornton do something more thrilling: retrieve 400 kilograms of cocaine from a drug cartel in Columbia.

Once the plane landed safely in a swamp in Montería, it was quickly surrounded by machine-gun-toting men. While Leonard ate what he later learned was a parrot, he watched Thornton load their transport. The illegal, addictive white powder was wrapped in yellow plastic bricks, packed into burlap, and then stuffed inside large duffel bags outfitted with parachutes. The value of their cargo on the return flight had increased by $80 million and one likely undercooked parrot.

As undigested bird rose in Leonard's throat, so did Leonard's ire. Angry over the betrayal, and teeming with salmonella, Leonard threw open the plane's door somewhere over Florida. And after returning the parrot's remains to the skies, Leonard kicked out three duffel bags of cocaine. Suddenly, the bird wasn't the only thing to disagree with Leonard. The two men began to fight. Their confrontation, however, was quickly interrupted by radio chatter. A Black Hawk helicopter and two DEA jets had spotted Thornton's Cessna as it crossed into U.S. air space. But Thornton had a plan.

Under the dim light of the cockpit, against the darkness of the night sky, Thornton strapped a parachute to himself. And during the roughly four minutes it took Thornton to affix a chute to Leonard, Thornton gave Leonard what would be his only skydiving lesson. After shoving three more duffel bags from the plane, Thornton lashed the remaining parcel to his person. Thornton barked instructions at Leonard, including that the pair would rendezvous at a hotel in Knoxville. With the plane on autopilot, they jumped.

On September 11, 1985, Fred Myers was finishing his morning shave, when he spied what appeared to be a man laying amidst debris in his driveway. Upon closer inspection, it was clear the crumpled person was dead; a trickle of dried blood ran from his mouth. Thornton had indeed landed in Knoxville, but not as he intended. Lifeless, Thornton was surrounded by the very things that had defined his life. He was wearing a bulletproof vest and special night vision goggles. He was carrying a Browning 9-mm automatic pistol, a .22-caliber pistol, and several clips of ammunition. He also had survival gear, a stiletto, and $4,500 in cash. And six gold Krugerrands, food rations, and vitamins. A compass, an altimeter, identification papers in two different names, and a membership card to the Miami Jockey Club. And, of course, a duffel bag filled with 77 pounds of cocaine. While it seemed Thornton's excessive gear may have played a role, police couldn't be sure why his parachute had failed him.

As the investigation continued, pieces of the mysterious puzzle began to come together. A crashed Cessna 404 was soon found nearby with no signs of fatalities and a number matching that on a key found among Thornton's things. Police ruled the death an accident—the cause: gravity—but the tale of the aviator was yet unknown. As the story became clearer, more duffel bags of cocaine were found in northern Georgia. But not before a particular black bear stumbled upon errant container.

When authorities finally discovered the bear's body on December 20, they also found 40 empty bags of cocaine. While the chief medical examiner who autopsied the animal found its stomach was "literally packed to the brim with cocaine," law enforcement wasn't certain whether the bear had consumed 75 pounds of the drug or some enterprising local had taken it. But the examiner was confident that after absorbing four grams of the substance, the bear had cerebral hemorrhaging, respiratory failure, hyperthermia, renal failure, heart failure, stroke and died shortly thereafter.

## 1999: THE ACCIDENTAL PROPHECY
### by Marcus Taylor

As the 20th century drew to a close, a digital threat known as the Y2K bug loomed over the world. This technological danger had its roots in the early days of computing, when programmers—seeking to conserve precious memory—abbreviated four-digit years to just two.

As the millennium approached, however, a realization dawned upon the world: the day after New Year's Eve 1999, computers might interpret the year "00" and not as 2000, but as 1900. As a result, it was believed, havoc would rein. Surely, banks would lose everyone's accounts. Airplanes would fall from of the sky. And worst of all—the world's nuclear arsenals, which were managed by computers, would undoubtedly fire off willy-nilly.

Almost 20 years earlier, long before anyone had even heard of a computer virus, the eventual countdown to midnight on December 31, 1999, was already part of the zeitgeist. In fact, it even had an anthem. "Two thousand zero zero...party over, oops, out of time." While Prince's "1999" was well-known when it ruled the radio, fans were unaware of how legendary filmmaker Orson Welles inspired the musician Prince to write the prophetic song. Perhaps even more fascinating are the similarities between the careers of these two artists.

Orson Welles wasn't exactly a fresh-faced newbie when Hollywood came a-knocking, but his fame stemmed from radio, not film. By 1938, Welles' booming voice and innovative adaptations, as featured on "Mercury Theatre on Air," had established Welles as a wunderkind. In October of that year, the day before Halloween, Welles shocked the nation with his radio adaptation of H.G. Wells' *The War of the Worlds*. So convincing, the hyper-realistic news bulletin caused widespread panic, and transformed the 23-year-old Welles into an instant celebrity. But was the young man ready to be thrust into the spotlight?

Prince wasn't exactly a fresh-faced newbie when record labels came a-knocking. By the time he was 13, he had formed his first band. The young musician quickly became a commanding fixture in Minneapolis' music scene, playing at community centers, proms and homecoming dances across Minneapolis. By the time he dropped out of school at 16, he had already laid the foundation for what would become the "Minneapolis Sound."

Confident he had what it took to be land a record deal, he flew to New York City. But his trip was unsuccessful. While he was away, however, a demo of a song he had created with producer Chris Moon made its way to the office of veteran promoter Owen Husney. That track would ultimately be his first single "Soft and Wet."

George J. Schaefer, head of RKO Pictures, saw an opportunity. He believed Welles' newly minted celebrity and talent for grabbing an audience's attention could translate to box office gold. Despite Welles' lack of film experience, Schaefer pursued him relentlessly through 1939.

Hollywood studios, at the time, were known for their tight control over filmmakers. RKO, however, was in a unique position—flush with cash and looking to make a name for themselves. This confluence of factors led to an unprecedented three film contract that gave newbie Welles the freedom to develop his own projects, assemble his own team, and be granted the power every director sought: final cut.

"I was immediately struck that this was something different," Owen Husney recounted of Prince. "I turned to Chris [Moon] and I said, 'So, who's the band here?' And he said, 'Well, Owen, it's not really a band.' And I thought, 'Oh no, is it a bunch of studio musicians? Because I don't really want to work with studio musicians; they can't tour.' And he said, 'No, it's not a studio band. It's one kid. He's just turned 18, and he's singing everything and playing all the instruments."

Recognizing Prince's potential, Husney didn't hesitate. After signing a management deal, Husney set up meetings in Los Angeles with Warner Bros., A&M, and Columbia. Within a week, all three labels were bidding for Prince. And within a month, less than three weeks after Prince's 19th birthday, Husney had negotiated the largest record deal for an untested artist in modern rock history. Like Welles before him, that contract included unprecedented artistic control for a first-time artist.

RKO's gamble on Welles opened with very mixed results. Following two aborted attempts to get a project off the ground, Welles finally released *Citizen Kane* in 1941. Despite its critical acclaim, and status as a cinematic milestone, the film struggled at the box office. Ultimately, it failed to recover its massive production costs.

Welles' controversial choice to portray a character inspired by media magnate William Randolph Hearst led to significant backlash. The Hearst organization launched a campaign to undermine the film and Welles. Their efforts included blackmail, red-baiting, and a push to have RKO destroy the film.

Although the Hearst press banned mentions of *Citizen Kane*, their actions ironically heightened interest elsewhere. Critics loved it. Despite widespread critical praise, however, the film faced significant resistance. Theaters in key cities, like New York and Los Angeles, refused to screen it, cementing its status as both a landmark achievement and a historic financial flop.

Warner Bros.' gamble on Prince paid off almost immediately. The prolific artist released an album every year each with more critical, sales and chart success than the last. Prince's first four albums laid the groundwork for his future stardom. While they showcased his talent, however, they didn't achieve mainstream success.

The first two—*For You* (1978) and *Prince* (1979)—barely cracked the Billboard Top 200, but included singles that gained some traction on the R&B and Dance charts. The next two—*Dirty Mind* (1980) and *Controversy* (1981)—continued to push boundaries while solidifying Prince's presence on those niche rankings. Although Prince's first four albums established him as a rising talent, widespread mainstream recognition continued to elude him.

> With *Citizen Kane* having run significantly over budget—one it did not recoup at the box office—Welles' contract was renegotiated. In the new terms, Welles lost his power, leaving studios to routinely meddle with his films. When Welles submitted his second movie, *The Magnificent Ambersons*, RKO cut more than 40 minutes and shot a completely new ending without Welles. When Welles learned his creation was butchered by the studio, he was furious.
>
> In truth, however, Welles had left for South America before *Ambersons* was complete. Instead, he began shooting a "semi-documentary" that RKO would shut down after it too ran over budget. Welles, and the executive who first hired him, were shown the door.

By the time Prince was scheduled to open for The Rolling Stones in October of 1981, he had built a loyal following. His distinct glam mashup of funk, R&B, and rock, however, was marketed primarily to African American audiences and radio stations. So, his successes were mostly limited to the dance and R&B charts. By this time, Rolling Stones' concerts had long been associated with violence, intolerance, and overall shenanigans. Prince's first night opening for them at the Coliseum would be no different

The mostly white audience, filled with Hell's Angels, was unimpressed by the colorful, funk-laced tunes from a showman that didn't conform to their macho ideals. Almost immediately, they started hurling a barrage of fried chicken, bottles, and other objects. And then, the requisite wave of racist and homophobic slurs followed. Prince and his band were only able to fight through four songs before having to run for cover.

After Prince's disastrous performance with the Stones, however, Mick Jagger personally asked The Purple One to rejoin the band at their next tour date two days later. Prince agreed. But unfortunately, the results were the same. While he was shaken, instead of shrinking, Prince headed back to what he did best: creating music. He'd come away from the incident even more determined to expand his audience so that he could headline his own arena shows.

In his 2006 book *Whatever Happened to Orson Welles?*, Joseph McBride wrote: "Unlike John Huston, who didn't balk at directing mediocre movies for hire in order to remain bankable, Welles was heroically unwilling to compromise as a director, but he was willing to do almost anything as an actor." By the 1970s, Welles—who had been living well beyond his means—was taking any job he could to pay the IRS.

His most famous pitches were for Paul Masson, that would famously "sell no wine before its time." Since many believed that this kind of work was beneath a man of such talent, he was often mocked. But Orson Welles famously defended the work saying, "It's the most innocent form of whoring I know." And Welles was good at it.

Along with hawking wine, Welles pitched spring water, airlines, cameras, board games, photocopiers, amusement parks, pay-per-view services, candy bars, and tires. Welles' baritone made him a voiceover favorite for other projects that took themselves way too seriously, including: The Alan Parsons Project's *Tales of Mystery and Imagination*, *Star Trek: The Motion Picture*, and 1978's *Lord of the Rings*.

And while many products leveraged the gravitas of the actor's voice, others used it ironically for films like *Revenge of the Nerds* and *The Muppets Take Manhattan*. Welles' unmistakable delivery, however, was best suited to the dozens of educational films he narrated, including the documentary that would help change the trajectory of Prince's career.

Following the Rolling Stones debacle, Prince was determined to build a following that would insure he would never again be an opening act. Due to the success of his early albums, Prince had enough money to experiment with his music. He acquired new drum machines and synthesizers to create a signature sound, one unlike anything previously heard. His efforts culminated in a record that would showcase what was to come. It was two-discs of all the things Prince had been longing to do musically since his raw demo in Minneapolis.

But while the LP contained a number of promising tracks—including the hit-in-waiting "Little Red Corvette"—it was missing a song that pulled the album together. Yet, Prince couldn't have anticipated where inspiration for that missing hit would strike.

It was the Fall of 1981. While promoting the album *Controversy* throughout the southern states of the U.S., Prince and his band The Revolution found themselves in need of overnight lodging. While they had been living the rock and roll life, one vice had eluded them: premium cable.

So, tempted by the promise of free HBO, a significant perk at the time, they chose one particular motel for their stay. And while Prince was notoriously frugal, on this particular evening, he allowed each band member to have their own room. Despite their separation, as if predetermined, they were all drawn to the movie playing on the Home Box Office. It was *The Man Who Saw Tomorrow*. And as fortune would have it, of the many documentaries exploring the 16th century prophecies of Nostradamus, this particular film was narrated by Orson Welles.

On the ride to the concert hall the next day, the Revolution discussed the curious film. But not Prince. He was missing. Arriving at their destination, the band found the musician already waiting there. In his hand, he held a cassette of a new song he was eager to share with his bandmates.

Prince had also watched the documentary. And one of Nostradamus's visions, as relayed by Orson Welles, had struck a chord. Literally. Drummer Bobby Z later reflected on the moment saying, "there explains the difference between mere mortals and Prince." While the band had simply watched the documentary, it had inspired Prince to compose a track overnight.

Prince's new composition merged an apocalyptic prophecy with a party counting down to doomsday. It was the missing piece. And as both the opening song and title track of Prince's fledgling new album, it would ultimately propel Prince's shining star to the heavens. And in a turn even Nostradamus could not predict, the track not only became a hit upon its release in 1982, but would become an anthem for a critical moment decades later.

That song, of course, was "1999."

## THE RENDLESHAM INCIDENT

December 29, 1980. Suffolk, England. As he did many mornings, Vince Thurkettle was chopping wood in Rendlesham Forest when a car screeched to a halt nearby. From out of the vehicle, two men dressed in suits appeared.

"Good morning," said one, in a well-spoken English accent. "Do you mind if we ask you some questions?" Once Thurkettle agreed, the stranger continued, "Were you out last night?"

"No," Thurkettle replied.

And at that, the pair thanked Thurkettle and left as quickly as they had arrived. Curious about the subject of the unusual inquiry, Thurkettle checked the local newspapers for the next few days. But he learned nothing. And the mystery wasn't revealed until three years later, when a *News of the World* headline announced: "UFO LANDS IN SUFFOLK."

While the world only learned of the apparent extraterrestrial incident in 1983, paranormal investigator Brenda Butler knew about it two days after Thurkettle received his strange visitors. On January 2, 1981, an informant contacted Butler with a story that piqued her particular interest. A strange aircraft had crashed in the forest of

Rendlesham. Two U.S. Air Force servicemen, who were stationed at the nearly Royal Air Force Base, were dispatched to investigate. Upon arriving, they observed that the unusual-looking craft was desperately in need of repairs. More curiously, the apparent vehicle, which seemed to be abuzz with energy, made no sound.

By the time Butler had learned of the bizarre incident in Rendlesham, she had been investigating the paranormal for nearly two decades. But her experience with the phenomena began many years before that.

While playing outside, at the mere age of five, Butler had witnessed a large, silvery craft—which she described as an "enormous bicycle wheel"—hovering in the sky. By age 12, she began to receive visits from short grey beings, with spindly appendages, and bulbous heads. While some would dismiss these experiences as the products of a youthful imagination, Butler claimed her parents bore witness too. Sadly, one such experience preceded the tragic death of her father.

In 1979, Butler was awoken in the early morning hours by a beam of light penetrating her bedroom window. Outside, she discovered the source. A large, white object hovered over the meadow adjacent to her home. On the ground below, stood a tall figure that donned long, golden hair and one-piece, silver uniform. Suddenly, a voice sounded within inside Butler's head. "Do not be afraid," it spoke. "I am not here to hurt you."

Brenda awoke the next day to a bad headache and the voice of her father talking about his experience the night before. It was identical to that of hers. But when Butler questioned him further, he forgot everything. It was as if his memory had been erased. And two months later, he died from a brain hemorrhage.

In January 1981, Butler was thrilled to learn of the downed craft from her mystery informant. Few were better suited to uncover the truth about the crash. Immediately, Butler began speaking with as many who may have had knowledge of the clandestine event. But after interviewing more than 200 people, she had documented a variety of different accounts. Some believed a UFO had crashed, tossing its dead, alien passengers outside the craft. But others reported seeing a Stealth Bomber forced to make an emergency landing. It wasn't until three years later, that Butler would learn in black and white what had occurred. For not only had airmen with the U.S. Air Force witnessed the event, but they had also documented it.

Sometime in July 1983, courtesy of her network of truth seekers, Butler received a memo issued on the letterhead of the U.S. Air Force dated January 13, 1981—was just two week after the Rendlesham Incident. Signed by a Colonel Charles Halt, it detailed the 24 hours Halt and his men had observed something inexplicable in the woods outside their England base. It was addressed to the Air Force's English counterparts at the Ministry of Defense. The understated subject: "Unexplained Lights."

The memo explained that in the early hours of December 27, 1980, two Air Force patrolmen raced their jeep toward an aircraft of some kind moving slowly through the trees. Multicolored beams of lights emanated from the source, which became obscured by the woods. When the forest grew impassable, the airmen abandoned their vehicle and continued on foot. And as they neared the locus of the flashing lights, the air became statically charged and dense. It was, they described, as if they were moving through "molasses." When they finally reached their destination, the patrolmen found it was not a downed aircraft, as they had suspected. Instead, it was something far more peculiar. And it was hovering.

Appearing to float above the undergrowth, the triangular-shaped craft was about the size of a tank. A red light sat atop its glossy black surface, and a bank of blue lights glowed from underneath. It was nothing like the veteran patrolmen had seen before. As Patrol Sergeant Jim Penniston approached the object, he saw what appeared to be hieroglyphs embedded upon its otherwise smooth exterior. But as he began to draw these strange symbols on his notepad, his movements became sluggish and labored. Penniston felt as if the energy was being drained from his body. After both men stepped back, the confounding vessel suddenly ascended into the sky and vanished.

Two days later, Colonel Charles Halt was enjoying Christmas dinner with other officers, when he was informed about what his airmen had found. After excusing himself, Halt gathered a few men and set out for the woods. Soon, they discovered the spot of the once downed craft and set up lights to aid their investigation. Three circular depressions in a triangular pattern were all that remained. A Geiger counter revealed that slightly elevated levels of radiation were most concentrated in the 7-inch diameter holes and on the ground at the intersection of the shapes. While the airmen continued their examination, the bedazzling light show reappeared. A red sun-like glow burned brightly through the trees, pulsing as it rose in the sky. The troops froze. Suddenly, the ascending shape broke into five separate white objects and then disappeared. But that was only the beginning.

As Colonel Halt and his men looked on in stunned silence, the lights that illuminated the crash site began to dim. Then, as Halt reported in his memo, three star-shaped objects appeared in the sky, two in the north and another in the south. "The objects moved rapidly in sharp angular movements, and displayed red, green and blue lights." While the unidentified flying objects first appeared elliptical, they soon morphed into full circles. The objects to the north remained sky bound for an hour before vanishing. The object in the south, which was visible for at least three hours, "beamed down a stream of light from time to time." The apparent target of the craft was a nearby weapons storage facility, which held a mystery of its own. It secretly housed nuclear missiles.

In August 1983, shortly after receiving Halt's memo, Butler contacted the Air Force Colonel. Although he was angry that the document had been leaked, he agreed to meet with the paranormal detective. During their meeting, Butler reported that Halt was "evasive, mysterious" and "shifty." When confronted about the details that appeared in the news that were noticeably absent from Halt's memo, Halt laughed. No creatures, he insisted, had been observed. But, he concluded, it was for Butler to determine the truth. And so, she did. But while Butler raced to complete a book documenting her research, others began to poke Uranus-sized holes in the story.

In January 1981, Simon Weeden was working for the Ministry of Defense (MOD) when he received Colonel Halt's memo entitled "Unexplained Lights." While Weeden routinely received reports of unusual skyward activity, this one was unique. It was from a military source.

Immediately, Weeden queried all of the MOD's radar stations. At least one must have detected the aircraft described in the memorandum. But after each reviewed their logs for the time in question, nothing had been seen on radar. Weeden concluded "no further action was necessary." And while the U.S. and English military looked to the sky, others believed they had found the lights' earthbound source.

On October 7, 1983, just days after the tabloid paper *News of the World* proclaimed a UFO had landed in Suffolk, journalist Ian Ridpath began investigating the incident. Soon, Ridpath spoke with Vince Thurkettle, who lived less than a mile from the purported landing site. When asked for the local opinion on the matter, Thurkettle said, "I don't know of anyone around here who believes that anything strange happened that night." Instead, he provided a practical explanation for what the airmen claimed to have seen in the woods. "It's the lighthouse," he said. Thurkettle explained that airmen were looking straight into the beam of the Orford Ness lighthouse.

This run-of-the-mill explanation, however, didn't satisfy everyone. Butler dismissed the theory because it didn't account for the physical object or the multi-colored lights the airmen had observed. On the other hand, Air Force security guard John Burroughs, who had witnessed the unusual event, believes the lighthouse did indeed play a role, but not in the way one might expect. Instead, Burroughs claims the lighthouse was emitting electromagnetic frequencies towards Rendlesham Forest. The airman believed he saw "plasma [energy], which could be a form of intelligence." And in his 2020 book *Weaponization of an Unidentified Aerial Phenomenon*, David Clarke concurred. He claimed the incident was caused by experiments in harnessing an energy field in the forest. None of these theses, however, explained the origin of the Yeti.

Even after she published her book *Sky Crash: A Cosmic Conspiracy* in 1984, Brenda Butler continued to investigate the Rendlesham Incident. During that time, some anonymous whistleblowers came forward to explain that purported alien aircraft was actually a Russian plane. The UFO story had been a cover up, they said. Many others, however, continued to witness extraterrestrial phenomenon in the woods there. And some, described a bear-like creature, standing at approximately nine feet in height, rummaging through the forest. A foul stench was said to precede the being, which made roaring noises as it traveled. According to Butler, Yetis are often spotted after the arrival of a UFO. And perhaps Rendlesham, she suggested, is home to an interdimensional portal.

With the benefit of time, Butler came to believe that the craft that crashed in Rendlesham was a Russian satellite. But she also conceded that "there has been such a big cover-up, nobody will ever know what happened." And while answers have not come from the government, they may have come from the strange visitors themselves. Patrol Sergeant Jim Penniston, who had allegedly documented the hieroglyphs on the downed UFO, consistently denied the ship was extraterrestrial. But after undergoing regression hypnosis in September of 1994, Penniston told his therapist the UFO was not from space, but time. The ship had delivered beings from thousands of years in the Earth's future. Regarding the beings, Penniston said, "They are us."

In September 1994, Penniston told his hypnotist that the craft he had observed years earlier contained our distant descendants. They had returned, Penniston explained, to obtain genetic material needed to keep their ailing species alive. Curiously, a year earlier, however, the made-for-TV movie *Official Denial* was broadcast on the Sci Fi channel. In it, an alien craft is shot by the U.S. Air Force, bringing it down in a forest. According to the film, the ship contained creatures that were here to "get genetic material to help them reproduce because their race is dying out." And the protagonist of the movie proclaimed they were not extraterrestrials saying, "They're us."

We may never know what transpired those two evenings in Rendlesham. Was it an extraterrestrial ship or a Russian plane? Was it a time machine or interdimensional portal?

Today, you may visit the woods in Suffolk. The forest even has its own official UFO trail, complete with a life-size replica of a flying saucer. But according to Brenda Butler, there are "eight landing sites down [there]. Everybody has got their own take on it. If you go down there with any of the witnesses, they'll take you somewhere else." And so, the clues to the Rendlesham Incident are just like the many UFO trails in Rendlesham, we're not sure which leads to the truth.

## RAPPER'S DELIGHT: THESE ARE THE GOOD CRIMES

In January of 1980, just one week into what would be a decade full of firsts, the Billboard 100 would memorialize "Rapper's Delight" as the first hip-hop track to hit the prestigious Billboard Top 40. After nine weeks of dominating radios and clubs, the song climbed steadily from number 84 to number 36. But the jubilance evoked by the popular jam was in contrast to its cynical creation. While the lighthearted lyrics of the song celebrate hotels, motels, and buttered toast, the behind-the-scenes story is one of unacknowledged talent, stolen art, and pilfered royalties.

By 1979, Sylvia Robinson's career in music played out like a warped record; two decades of highs and lows. But after a string of setbacks, Robinson's first record label appeared to be fading out. All Platinum records had collapsed.

It was in the midst of this tumult that Robinson visited Harlem World, one of the few New York spots to bring the burgeoning street culture of beats and rhymes indoors. Arriving for a party, she was floored by the sight of DJ Lovebug Starski rapping over the break from the hit of the summer, Chic's "Good Times." Fresh from a religious retreat to salve her burdened soul, Robinson decided that she had found her deliverance. Something, perhaps the voice of God, she believed, told her: put this music on wax.

Curiously, Robinson had a similar experience twenty years earlier.

By 1956, Sylvia Robinson was already poised to be a music icon. A rising star, she and her music partner, Mickey Baker, shared a bill with Bo Diddley at a concert in Washington, D.C. From backstage at the Howard Theatre, the duo watched Diddley perform with guitarist Jody Williams, who played a captivating riff. Inspired, Robinson and Baker asked Diddley for permission to use the melody in a new song. With Diddley's blessing, Baker and Robinson, who performed as Mickey & Sylvia, recorded "Love is Strange." Released in November of 1956, it became their biggest hit. It dominated the charts, sold more than a million copies and was certified gold.

In 1956, however, there was a problem with Diddley's approval. He didn't write the music alone. Indeed, the guitar line that had so enthralled Mickey & Sylvia was composed by the very guitar virtuoso they had witnessed playing on that Washington, DC, stage.

In 2012, Williams recalled:

I remember playing onstage…and seeing…movement behind the curtain. [There] I see Mickey Baker, stealing all he can get. Bo ended up letting Mickey and Sylvia have that song. To this day, I haven't seen a dime of that money.

Although he eventually filed a lawsuit, Williams lost the case. And following that experience, the promising guitarist abandoned his musical career. Sadly for Williams, in 1987 the song's popularity resurged, when it appeared in one of the most successful films of that year—and on the movie's companion album, which at fourteen times platinum, is one of the biggest-selling soundtracks of all time. The movie was *Dirty Dancing*.

"Love Is Strange" gave Sylvia Robinson a hit that proved impossible to follow. Fortunately, Robinson had the talent and the ability for a plan B based in songwriting and production. Unfortunately, there was little precedent for a woman in that role. And in what was most likely the result of sexism—or perhaps karmic retribution failing Jody Williams—Robinson's own early production work, which included a Grammy-nominated song for Ike and Tina Turner, went uncredited.

Being denied recognition throughout her secondary career may have fueled Robinson's drive in the decades that followed. But her successes did not satisfy her hunger for acknowledgement. Instead, her ambitions evolved into greed and tarnished her reputation.

In 1968, Sylvia and her then-husband Joe leveraged Sylvia's experience, and some alleged mob investments, to create All Platinum Records. Sylvia built the roster, signing groups like The Moments, while Joe handled the operations and scavenged for projects to promote. Their combination of intellect and intuition garnered a string of classic soul hits for the new record label.

In the mid-1970s, All Platinum made an expansion play for the venerated Chess Records catalog. But when the Robinsons couldn't monetize the assets, that partnership ended in litigation. Compounding their troubles, Joe's under-the-table dealings resulted in a payola investigation and a conviction for tax evasion that drove All Platinum's artists to flee rather than forfeit their careers. And by the end of the decade, All Platinum had filed for bankruptcy.

It was this confluence of events that found Robinson staring uncomfortably at DJ Lovebug Starski at that hip-hop party at Harlem World in 1979. Without hesitation, Robinson sent her niece Diane to the DJ booth to tell Starski that she'd like to record him. Bewildered by the request, Starski flatly refused. Undeterred, Sylvia contacted the performer after the show. But Starski again rejected the offer, reluctant to do business with Robinson because of her rumored underworld ties.

Returning to her home across the Hudson River, Robinson began searching for what she learned was called a rapper. It was this quest, and not an empty stomach, that led Robinson to Crispy Crust Pizza on West Palisade Avenue in Englewood, New Jersey.

Rumor had it, that in addition to slices, one employee at Crispy Crust Pizza was serving up hot and fresh rhymes. As she entered the pizzeria, Robinson spied one particularly large employee rapping along to a song playing on a boombox perched nearby. Impressed, Robinson invited the young man, who she would come to know as "Big Bank" Hank Jackson, to audition for her in the Oldsmobile 98 parked outside.

And as fortune would have it, Guy "Master Gee" O'Brien walked by during Jackson's trial and tossed his name (and rhymes) into the hat. Thrilled, Robinson invited them to her mansion for further discussion. There, they were joined by "Wonder Mike" Wright, a homeless man who had been rapping for just two months when had heard of Robinson's auditions. And while Robinson intended to sign only one rapper, she was unable to choose. So, she instead dubbed the entire trio The Sugarhill Gang.

With rappers in place, Robinson was missing a critical element: the music. And while she may not have understood how Starski's live backing track was created, she knew she needed one long version of an instrumental to serve as the bed for her new music group. To emulate the technique pioneered by DJ Kool Herc years earlier—one that could extend the break of a song ad infinitum—Robinson did what she had done for countless previous tracks. She employed a band.

Robinson directed Positive Force, recent signees to her nascent Sugar Hill Records, to lay down an instrumental track. And while they would parrot a hit song, the performance demanded by Robinson would differ than that of original band's in two ways. One was imperceptible, another was unmistakable.

Having decided to forgo college in 1979, seventeen-year-old Chip Shearin traveled from his North Carolina home to visit a friend in New Jersey. Once there, Shearin's friend invited him to tour the Sugar Hill production studio that employed him. While Shearin was fascinated to see how records were pressed into vinyl, the skilled bass player became part of the record-producing machine itself.

As it turned out, Robinson needed a bassist. Upon learning Shearing fit the bill, she asked him if he could play "Good Times." A fan of Chic bassist Bernard Edwards, Shearin answered in the affirmative. Grateful, Robinson then asked Shearin if he could play it, but slightly differently. Uncertain about this unusual request, Shearin agreed. He would play the infamous riff on the "downbeat rather than the upbeat."

"And," Robinson added, "I need you to play it for fifteen minutes without interruption."

Just days later, the Sugarhill Gang stepped up to the microphones, and after only one take, "Rapper's Delight" was complete. Refusing to edit the fifteen-minute track for length, Robinson found it difficult to find a radio station willing to play it. Finally, Jim Gates, a jock at WESL, in St. Louis, spun the lengthy song, and success immediately followed.

While orders flooded the small NJ record label, stations throughout the country began playing the track. At its peak, production hustled to press more than 50,000 copies per day. And with two million units sold within just a few weeks, the song reach number 36 on the Top 40, the first hip-hop record to do so.

But the overwhelming success also brought some unwanted attention from those from whom the song had been stolen.

On September 20, 1979, Chic performed a concert at New York disco Bond's with new wave band Blondie. Also present, was future name-check in Blondie's "Rapture," Fab 5 Freddy. And when Bernard Edwards finally dropped the bass line to "Good Times," Freddy seized the stage to rap, surprising the band and thrilling the audience. Chic founding member Nile Rodgers, who had only witnessed rap for the first time weeks earlier, was equally charmed.

Shortly thereafter, however, Rodgers' opinion changed. Just a few months later, while visiting the midtown Manhattan dance club Leviticus, Rodgers was excited to hear the opening bass line of his hit blasting through the hall's speakers. But when Rodgers heard Wonder Mike's now iconic opening line, Rodgers was enraged. What he heard was "not a test."

Rodgers and Chic bassist Bernard Edwards quickly contacted their lawyer. And when the Robinsons scoffed at a deal to settle the matter, Sugar Hill's chief investor, Morris Levy—who had ties to the Genovese crime family, and was later convicted of extortion—intervened. Ultimately, a settlement avoided a trial and gave Rodgers and Edwards writing credits and, more importantly, royalties. Not everyone from whom Sugar Hill stole, however, was so lucky.

Even though it was a mainstream success, the consensus from uptown rhyme purists was that the popular track was a joke. The group's labelmate Melle Mel, of the celebrated Grandmaster Flash and the Furious Five, dismissed the Sugarhill Gang as fake Garden State interlopers. Worst of all, one of the rappers featured on the breakthrough track had committed high treason in the hip-hop community. He had stolen another's rhymes.

In 1979, before the release of "Rapper's Delight," the hip-hop pioneer Grandmaster Caz, who went by DJ Casanova Fly at the time, was the leader of the Mighty Force crew. Noting that other rap acts, like Funky 4+1 and Grandmaster Flash, had managers who helped them book gigs, Caz sought representation. He offered the role to the bouncer, whom he had befriended at a hip-hop club in the Bronx. And Hank Jackson accepted.

Success on his mind, Jackson immediately borrowed money from his parents to purchase a sound system for his new business. To repay the parental loan, however, Jackson took another job, one closer to his home—one at Crispy Crust Pizza in Englewood, NJ.

Excited about his new managerial prospect, "Big Bank" Hank Jackson brought two items to work each day: a boombox and a cassette featuring his clients, DJ Casanova Fly and the Mighty Force. While slicing pizza pies into eight rather similarly sized pieces, Jackson rapped along to the lyrics spit by Caz on the tape.

It was there that Sylvia Robinson first saw Big Bank Hank performing, only she didn't realize that he was singing along with another's rhymes. And she may have never known, in spite of one, very obvious clue.

While Master Gee spelled his name out in Rapper's Delight (as was and is the practice of many rappers), Jackson—who went by Big Hank—

spelled out C-A-S-A-N-O-V-A F-L-Y, the moniker of his client. And while Sylvia Robinson is credited on the hit as a songwriter, something she did with all of her acts, Grandmaster Caz is not.

In spite of its detractors, Sugar Hill Records was on top. Any street cred the label may have initially lost, was earned quickly with the release of 1981's groundbreaking "The Adventures of Grandmaster Flash on the Wheels of Steel," the first record to showcase the turntablism that has become a hallmark of hip-hop. And by 1982, Sugar Hill's roster included rap pioneers like Melle Mel, the Treacherous Three, the Funky 4+1, and Spoonie Gee.

Soon, the first-of-its-kind Sugar Hill Revue hit the road on an international tour. Robinsons' artists, which also included gold-selling trio The Sequence, were now opening arena gigs for R&B and funk stars the O'Jays, Parliament-Funkadelic, and Rick James. But the label's momentum quickly cratered.

With the overwhelming success of the genre-creating "Rapper's Delight," the industry Robinson had built was hers to lose. And following a series of bad financial deals, and a pattern and practice of swindling her artists, that is precisely what she did.

Not included in any of the group's profits or royalties, the trio who helped launch the label was no better off than before they had "up jumped the boogie" to the beat. Within about five years of traveling the world, Wonder Mike was forced to paint houses to make ends meet, while Master Gee was penniless. And while she may not have been empathetic, a series of lawsuits would teach Robinson how being broke is no joke. And how it's "hard as hell to fight it."

While "Rapper's Delight" interpolated "Good Times," to the ultimate fortune of Chic's founder, Melle Mel's "White Lines" went further. That track, which reached number five on Billboard's dance chart, borrowed the melody, music and lyrics from Liquid Liquid's "Cavern." Like Nile Rodgers before them, the band sued, only with different results. When death threats against the owner of the band's record label failed (which may have included a machete), the case dragged on for fifteen months. And while the court ultimately awarded the plaintiffs $660 in damages and legal fees, Sugar Hill filed for bankruptcy before being forced to pay—just one day after the IRS moved to seize the label's assets for the alleged non-payment of more than $200,000 in payroll taxes. Indeed, the "money gets divided."

As their underhanded financial dealings tarnished their reputation, an evolving landscape led by the harder beats-and-rhymes swagger of Run-D.M.C. pushed Sugar Hill to the brink. Def Jam Records, with its growing all-star roster that included LL Cool J, Beastie Boys and Public Enemy, made the New Jersey label obsolete. And after 26 gold records, the Robinsons lifted the needle off of Sugar Hill in 1986.

In 2011, nearly a decade after Joe had passed, Sylvia Robinson died at age 76. Ten years later, she was voted into the Rock & Roll Hall of Fame, joining her former artists Grandmaster Flash and the Furious

Five, which became the first rap group inducted into the Rock Hall in 2007.

## THE MONSTER WITH 21 FACES

It was March 18, 1984. Although the sun had set a few hours earlier on the city of Nishinomiya, Japan, two men had just begun their nefarious work. With guns in hand, the soon-to-be criminals stood just outside the front door of 70-year-old Yoshie Ezaki. As the elderly woman began her nighttime ablutions, the men, their faces obscured by white ski masks, burst in. Easily subduing the frail Yoshie, the pair bound her with a severed telephone cord. But to her great fortune their only interest was in a single, tiny item in her possession: the key to the home of her son, Katsuhisa Ezaki.

Moments after terrorizing Yoshie, the evil duo slunk through the dark of night to the home next door, the dwelling of Katsuhisa Ezaki, the president of the Glico company. Using the stolen key, the masked gunmen quietly entered the house before them. But the quiet did not last long. Soon, a shriek erupted from Ezaki's stunned wife as she clung to her eldest daughter.

"Take our money," she pleaded, "but leave us alone."

"Your money is meaningless," came the response of one of the assailants. Then, after binding their new captives together, the burglars moved deeper into the labyrinthine home.

The two thugs crept throughout the home of Ezaki, the remaining residents unaware of their alarming presence. Opening one door, then another, they carefully checked each room along their path. Then, they found the other Ezaki children sleeping comfortably in their beds. But the sound of running water soon drew their attention to the end of the hall. There, the criminals found the head of the household, undressed and unaware, as he emerged from the bath. Immediately, the masked men were upon Ezaki, binding the naked man and shrouding his head in a canvas sack. Dragging him outside, the duo stuffed the Glico president into a waiting car, which sped into the darkness.

By sunrise the next morning, police had already been busy trying to determine the motivation for the abduction of Glico's president. Founded a century earlier by Ri-ichi Ezaki, Glico established itself quickly as a popular brand of confections. Their products, the company boasted, were made with health-boosting oyster glycogen. As the decades rolled on, Glico added new delights to its offerings. Then in 1966, Glico's introduced its now internationally renowned treat Pocky, the world's first chocolate covered biscuit sticks. In 1984, however, Glico was just a mid-size, mediocre food processor. That its owner would be targeted struck investigators as odd. But then a clue was found.

Just hours after Ezaki disappeared, a letter materialized. Discovered at a telephone booth near the Ezaki residence, the note requested $4.2 million for the safe return of the Glico president. While acquiring this sum would have been difficult, the next demand was nigh impossible.

The kidnappers also required 220 pounds of gold bullion, bringing the total of the demand to approximately $6 million. It was the largest ransom ever made in Japanese history. Determined to bring Ezaki home, the police spent the next three days searching for the missing man, while struggling with his captor's demands. But their investigation was interrupted by the appearance of barefoot man.

Although his feet were naked, the man was clothed, albeit with ill-fitting attire. He shambled across the street toward the officer on the opposite corner. The policeman was busy speaking with passersby, flashing a photo of Ezaki as they paused. Finally standing before the lawman, the barefoot stranger spoke with a weak voice, "I am the one you're looking for."

Once in police custody, Katsuhisa Ezaki detailed his 72-hour ordeal. Although a bag had been kept over his head during his captivity, his assailants had otherwise treated him humanely. They clothed the man, fed him crackers and did not harm him. When he was final able to loosen the ropes that bound him, Ezaki escaped. But his freedom didn't end his persecution from his mysterious captors.

"To the Japanese police, are you stupid?" A mysterious letter had been delivered to the police. "There's so many of you. What on earth are you doing? If you are real pros, try catching me. Since there's too much of handicap, I will give you a hint." The letter went on to include the following supposed clues: that the getaway vehicle in the abduction of Katsuhisa Ezaki was gray, and that the abductors had purchased food from a well-known supermarket chain. They further taunted the police by threatening, "Should we kidnap the head of the police?" The note was signed, "Kaijin nijuichi menso," which translates to "The Monster with 21 Faces."

About a month after the abduction, Ezaki, who had returned to his work at Glico, was leading another of his many routine meetings. Suddenly, one of Ezaki's assistants burst into the conference room, terror in her eyes. But before she could speak, one of the meeting's attendees shrieked, drawing Ezaki's view to a nearby window. Peering through the glass, Ezaki watched in horror as several vehicles in the parking lot below were engulfed in flames. Hurrying through the Glico facility—security now in tow—Ezaki came upon another astonishing sight. There inside the company building, employees had discovered a container full of hydrochloric acid. As the deadly vessel was discovered, an anonymous caller phoned Glico.

The call was direct. A one-time payment of approximately $1 million would bring Glico's torment to an end. After Ezaki refused to pay the demand, the police became more determined to find the culprits. The location of the deadly chemical led police to believe it was an inside job. Disgruntled employees were added to the growing list of suspects. But then, with the ransom unpaid, and the investigation ongoing, the true target of the Monster became clear. Letters began arriving at media outlets throughout Osaka. For years, Glico had touted their food products as wholesome and health-boosting. Now, Glico's confections, the screeds suggested, were now deadly. They had been laced with cyanide.

Following the May 1984 letters, panic erupted across Japan. Retailers everywhere pulled Glico products from their shelves. Supermarkets urged citizens to return any confections they may have at home. Yet after the dust from the ensuing chaos settled, not a single trace of a toxin was found in any of the Glico products. Nevertheless, the damage had been done. The stunt took a toll on the company's bottom line. Ezaki predicted the year's sales would be off by about $130 million. Glico was forced to lay off 1,000 employees. But this was enough to satisfy The Monster with 21 Faces, who forgave the manufacturer. In June of 1984, the Monster announced the surprising turn in another letter to the press.

> To our fans throughout Japan: We're satisfied. The president of Glico has already gone around with his head hanging down low enough. We would like to forgive him. In our group there's a four-year old kid—every day he cries for Glico. It's a drag to make a kid cry because he's deprived of the candy he loves. So, we're also really upset. It would be great if we could forgive Glico, so the supermarkets could sell their products again.

In truth, although the Monster turned its sights away from Glico, it had already been harassing other food companies. And this time, it was prepared to make good on its threats.

In the weeks prior to ending its feud with Glico, The Monster with 21 Faces had already begun threatening the food company Marudai Ham. And on the same day they forgave Glico, the criminal group demanded Marudai executives pay $113,000 to avoid the criminals' wrath. Unlike Glico, Marudai agreed. But instead of sending an employee with the money, as the mysterious blackmailers had insisted, a policeman disguised as an employee followed the Monster's instructions and boarded a Kyoto-bound train.

As the train barreled north, the disguised officer scanned the terrain outside for the signal. A white flag would be hung somewhere. At that moment, the imposter-employee was to toss the ransom-filled sack out of the train window. But as the officer watched for his cue, he noticed a man watching him. A large man with short hair and eyes like those of a fox peered surreptitiously through his glasses at the officer. While being mindful of his audience, the officer continued to look outside. But by the time the train reached Kyoto, the white flag had never appeared, and the fox-eyed man had vanished. Having reached the end of the line, the officer caught the next train bound for home. But he wasn't the only one headed back to Osaka.

Exhausted and frustrated, the disguised police officer rose slowly as the train arrived back at Osaka. It was then that he noticed a familiar face. There at the other end of the car sat the bespectacled fox-eyed man. Their eyes connected just as the doors of the train opened. As the officer hurried toward the suspicious man, the man hurried from the train. And by the time the policeman reached the platform, the fox had eluded him. But it wouldn't be long before the police would have another chance to capture this curious suspect. Their next encounter, however, would have deadly consequences.

By October of 1984, The Monster with 21 Faces had added another food company to its who-to-extort list. The mysterious criminals had demanded $400,000 from Morinaga & Company. Unlike their other ransom demands, however, this letter from the Monster also included 30 grams of cyanide, a substance that is lethal, if consumed. That small, but deadly, quantity foreshadowed the scores of terror yet to come. For when the Morinaga Company refused to comply, an even more frightening note arrived at news agencies throughout the country.

To moms throughout Japan,

In Autumn, when appetites are strong, sweets are delicious. Well, we've added some special flavor. The flavor of cyanide is a little bitter. It won't cause tooth decay, so buy the sweets for your kids. We've put 20 boxes of Morinaga in stores from Hakata to Tokyo.

Once again, terror struck Japan. No longer was Osaka the sole target. Forty thousand police officers were mobilized throughout the country. And as the officers continued to search stores in cities across the nation they found what they were looking for: several packages of Morinaga Choco Balls and Angel Pies on shelves in Osaka, Kyoto, and a department store in Nagoya had a curious label affixed to them. It read: "Danger. Contains poison. You'll die if you eat this. The Monster with 21 Faces."

After this phase of the ordeal had ended, several packages were confirmed to contain lethal doses of cyanide. But the terrorists didn't wait for the authorities to finish their accounting. In the coming weeks, more letters arrived, each threatened a repeat offense with one change. The mysterious extortionists wrote: "Morinaga is the best when it comes to confections. But now their products taste a bit better since we have added a special seasoning of sodium cyanide."

This time, however, the Monster made it clear that the deadly packages would not carry a warning. It would be impossible to find the dangerous treats. A panic similar to that following the Glico threats ensued. Every Morinaga candy, biscuit, and cookie was pulled from store shelves. And though not a single poisoned confection was consumed, Morinaga's bottom line was harmed.

Meanwhile, after weeks of harassment, House Foods—yet another of the Monster's targets—agreed to pay $450,000 to rid themselves of their plight. So, on November 14, 1984, a House Foods employee followed the instructions the extortionists had given. The police likewise followed their orders and observed the employee from a safe distance. But as the worker with the money neared the drop-off location in the Shiga Prefecture, he could not find a garbage bin marked with a white cloth, the one in which he was to leave the ransom. Instead, a white cloth lay on the ground nearby, signaling that the Monster had called the deal off. But police everywhere were on high alert. So, it was no surprise when one officer spotted a familiar fox-eyed man, behind the wheel of a nearby car.

Once again, the police pursued their key suspect, this time in a vehicle. But as it was before, the phantom eluded law enforcement. A short time later, the police found the suspect's car abandoned at a nearby railroad station. Inside, they discovered how the Monster continued to evade authorities. There in the vehicle was a police scanner. Having confirmed their suspicions about the fox-eyed man, police released sketches of the suspect. This increased effort, however, could not lessen the shame of the officer leading the investigation that saw the Monster slip through its fingers. Humiliated, Superintendent Yamamoto of the Shiga Prefecture stepped into his backyard, doused himself with kerosene, and lit himself on fire. This, it seems, prompted one final act from the criminal mastermind.

The death of Superintendent Yamamoto prompted another correspondence from the Monster.

> No-career Yamamoto died like a man. So, we decided to give our condolences. We decided to forget about torturing food companies. We are bad guys which means we've got more to do than bullying companies. It's fun to lead a bad man's life.

After this, The Monster with 21 Faces was never heard from again. And nearly 40 years later, the identity of the person or people behind the criminal organization still remains a mystery.

## THE CABBAGE PATCH PATERNITY TEST

In November 1983, more than 1,000 people stood, gathered in the frigid air, just outside the Zayre's Department Store in Wilkes-Barre, Pennsylvania. Cold and anxious, the throng—many of whom had been waiting since midnight—began to shout for the store to open early. Taped inside the glass doors of the retail establishment, taunting the would-be customers, was the sign that had drawn them there: Cabbage Patch Kids – In Stock. And while the most shops had been selling the popular—albeit homely—dolls for $30, Zayre's was offering them for the low-low price of $17.99. But the prices weren't the only thing that would be knocked down that day.

After eyeing the now unruly mob, the assistant store manager positioned himself behind a counter, his legs wide, his hands firmly clutching a baseball bat. Finally, at 8:50 am, the manager unlocked the doors. Immediately, the once immobilized herd bull rushed their way inside, each hoping to nab a Cabbage Patch doll. In the frenzy, the otherwise civilized humans succumbed to their baser drives. One woman was knocked to the floor as she tried to hold onto a doll being snatched from her hands by a man. Another woman clung to one of the toys as another woman choked her with a purse strap. During the stampede, the assistant manager jumped on the counter before him, swinging his bat, demanding the crowd calm down.

As five women—their bones broken—were being transported to Wilkes-Barre General Hospital, Cabbage Patch Kids were being birthed at Babyland General 750 miles south of Pennsylvania. And while disputes over dolls at Zayre's, and countless other stores across the United States, had left many bruised and battered, the Cabbage Patch Kids were the subject of an even bigger custody battle. The very parentage of the dolls was in question. At stake was $1 million and a broken heart.

Born in the two-red-lights town of Cleveland, Georgia, Xavier Roberts had never been a good student. So, poor both academically and financially, Roberts focused his junior college career on the one path that was all but guaranteed to keep him penniless—art. While studying his chosen field at school, Roberts supplemented the pittance he earned from his work at the state park by crafting pottery and selling his wares to his classmates. Then, one day in 1976, seven years before the trampling of customers in Zayre's, Roberts saw something that would change his life.

Roberts' aha moment, as told to the Washington Post in 1983, was a photo of a soft sculpture, the art form popularized in the 1960s. To his great advantage, Roberts already understood the technique; he had watched his mother make quilts as a side hustle. Inspired, Roberts began shaping four-way stretch fabric instead of clay. Soon—in what sounds like the premise to a horror movie—Roberts began sculpting his many nieces and nephews out of cloth, stuffing the dolls with soft fibers, stitching the mouths, painting their eyes. And although each one, as Roberts described, was different, each bore the signed name of their creator. It soon became clear, however, the dolls Roberts had begun fashioning were not as unique as he suggested.

According to Roberts' rag doll-to-riches tale, he began selling his creations at flea markets and craft fairs. In lieu of describing the intimate process of creating life, Roberts explained to his customers that he had found his babies in a cabbage patch. Roberts called them "Little People." To further distinguish his product from traditional dolls, Roberts told customers they were not for sale. Instead, they could be adopted. In fact, each doll came with a birth certificate bearing a one-of-a-kind name (gleaned from an actual 1938 Georgia birth registry). But as Roberts' Little People grew in popularity, it became clear that they weren't the only thing that were made out of whole cloth.

Born in 1950 and raised in the small town of Mayfield, Kentucky, Martha Nelson Thomas had long known that she wanted to be an artist. Ultimately leaving her humble home for the big lights of Louisville, Nelson attended the Louisville School of Art in the early 1970s. While studying her chosen field, Thomas eschewed the traditional media employed by her classmates. Instead, she began experimenting with something that would define her life: soft sculpture. Inspired by the children in her circle, Thomas shaped four-way stretch fabric into dolls, whom she thought of as babies. Stuffing each with soft fibers, stitching the mouths, painting their eyes, every baby Thomas "birthed," was unique. Unfortunately for Thomas, chicanery was commonplace.

By 1976, Martha Nelson Thomas had been making and selling her "Doll Babies" at craft fairs throughout Kentucky to some success. Not only were her soft-sculpted dolls one-of-a-kind, but her marketing approach was too. Buyers could not buy a doll, instead they could adopt a baby. Consistent with actual babies, Thomas' "children" bore no labels or tags. And adoptive parents received a birth certificate and papers identifying their uniquely named child and describing its interests. Her charming approach drew the attention of many enthusiastic customers and one cowboy-hat-wearing young man.

While attending a crafts fair in Berea, Kentucky, Thomas was approached by 21-year-old Xavier Roberts. Fascinated with her "Doll Babies," Roberts told Thomas he wanted to sell them at the gift shop at the state park he managed in Georgia. Intrigued, Thomas agreed. And after returning home with Doll Babies in tow, Roberts began selling Thomas' creations from his place of employ. Dissatisfied with the price Thomas had been charging, however, Roberts jacked up the cost to the consumer. But soon, when Thomas learned of Roberts' exorbitant "adoption fees," Thomas demanded that he return her dolls. And while Roberts complied with the request, he also sent a letter to Thomas saying that he would "carry your type of dolls, either made by you or someone else."

That someone else was Roberts. Assisted by three friends and his mother, Roberts' crew handcrafted dolls that looked in most respects like those created by Thomas. And while he didn't craft each personally, Roberts was sure to sign all of them. Each of the "Little People" bore the name of their alleged creator on their buttocks. And when the demand of for the toys exceeded his production capacity, Roberts purchased a derelict clinic, expanded his staff, and established the Babyland General Hospital. When a baby was born there, a nurse announced over a loudspeaker: "Cabbage dilation, all staff on standby!" Beneath the Magic Crystal Tree, doctors would inject the gaping vegetation with "Imagicillin" just before yanking a nude doll from the leafy womb.

By 1980, when word had spread about Roberts' apparently inventive dolls, not everyone attributed the toys to Roberts. While visiting Martha Nelson Thomas, who had continued to sell her brand of soft-sculpted babies at craft fairs in Kentucky, one confused patron congratulated the Thomas. The customer explained that she had seen Thomas' product being sold at an Atlanta airport. Thomas, of course, had not done so. And when she learned who was behind the knock offs, Thomas was heartbroken.

After some cajoling by friends, the otherwise shy, salt-of-the-earth artist sought counsel from legal aid, the only attorney she could afford. While Thomas had resigned herself to the life of a bohemian artist, she was devasted that her babies were being mass-produced. And soon, a lawsuit seeking $1 million was filed against Roberts. "I know we're asking for money," said Thomas, "but that's not the reason we're in it. It's not completely honest to sell his dolls, and then, when asked where it originated, to omit my part." But the case wouldn't be heard until years after Roberts had become a multi-millionaire.

By 1981, Atlanta entrepreneur Roger Schlaifer saw the billion-dollar potential of the Little People and sought to license the product. While Roberts was initially reluctant to do so, Schlaifer attempted to woo the "entrepreneur" with a mythology for the babies that placed Roberts at the center of the tale. For although vegetation routinely gave "birth" at Babyland General Hospital, Roberts offered no explanation as to their conception.

Instead of the male equivalents of a cabbage, BunnyBees—horrifying-sounding hybrids of rabbits and hornets—pollinated the cabbages by "dropping crystals on them." Fortunately, according to the lore spun by Schlaifer, 10-year-old Xavier Roberts, had followed a BunnyBee to the debaucherous garden of child-rearing. To save the newborns from the clutches of the evil Lavender McDade, young Roberts brought them to Babyland General so they may be adopted by a loving home. (Or purchased by a parent willing to throw down at a department store.) Roberts was sold on the marketing concept.

Schlaifer, who described Roberts' toys as "really ugly dolls," had won the license of the product. Rebranding the dolls, Schlaifer sold the "Cabbage Patch Kids" to Coleco, the toy company that was poised to have the country's second biggest hit of the season, the Adam computer.

While Roberts' dolls—and Thomas' before—were made entirely of cloth, Coleco utilized the latest in technology to sculpt the heads from vinyl. Aided by computers, Coleco factories could mass produce the toys, while still making each one different: varying the hair, eye and skin color, and dimples, freckles, and cheekbones. Barbara Wruck, Coleco's director of corporate communications, was thrilled, saying, "What a homely little thing."

In 1985, as sales of Cabbage Patch Kids and their related products raced toward $2 billion, Martha Nelson Thomas' lawsuit against Xavier Roberts was nearing its close. The case was divided into two parts: copyright and fair trade. After a copyright hearing in 1982, a federal district court judge ruled that the copyright Roberts had obtained was valid. Roberts, they concluded, had not misrepresented himself by not giving credit to Thomas. For her part, Thomas said she didn't know she needed a copyright. Likewise, she didn't put a brand name, or copyright insignia, on the dolls because she felt babies had no place for such things. Roberts, of course, had branded all of his babies.

The second half of the suit, focused on whether Roberts was in violation of federal law for claiming in advertisements that his product was "original." While Roberts' attorney conceded that Roberts got the idea for his dolls "partly from [Thomas]," he maintained Roberts' expression of the idea was quite different from that of Thomas. But Thomas' attorney disagreed. The differences, he asserted, if any, were slight. And yet, the odds were stacked against Thomas. Courts overhearing other similar disputes between Roberts and rival companies, made an example of Thomas' dolls, highlighting how they differed from those of Roberts. Thomas was fighting a losing battle. Then things changed.

Before the trial concluded, Roberts' attorney asked Thomas to settle out of court. Thomas longed to leave the conflict behind her and return to her work as an artist. So, that day, the parties came to an agreement. As a result, Thomas was able to provide some input in the doll production and received a monetary award. While that amount could not be disclosed, Thomas told her close friends that "her children would go to college." Likewise, Roberts, who by then was a multi-millionaire and a "most eligible bachelor," said he planned to return to school to learn how to become a sculptor. Possibly, for the first time.

## MASQUERADE
### by George W. Krubski

By March of 1976, Tom Maschler had an illustrious career at the British Publishing firm John Cape. One of his first assignments gave rise to Ernest Hemingway's memoir *A Moveable Feast*, he purchased the British rights to *Catch-22* for a pittance, and he shepherded books by Salman Rushdie and John Lennon. A force behind the United Kingdom's prestigious Booker Prize, Maschler had a talent for knowing not just what would sell, but what would sell well. Maschler needed a work that could exploit the growing market for lavishly illustrated children's books. It was this that led Maschler to a moss-covered cottage in rural Gloucestershire.

The door to the quaint home opened to reveal Kit Williams. An eccentric, solitary artist, Williams had a leprechaun's beard, a lazy eye, and a mad scientist's heart. Although he looked the part—and had built a television from scratch before his thirteenth birthday—Williams never found success in academics. Instead, he ran away to the Royal Navy, where he taught himself to paint to avoid playing cards with the other enlisted men. Machler was certain Williams was perfect artist for the job. But could Machler convince the lone creator to partner with a writer? No.

Williams wanted nothing to do with what Maschler was pitching—an illustrated children's book was beneath the quirky artist. Even more so, a partner would infringe on Williams' freedom to control every aspect of his work. Their meeting unsuccessful, Maschler headed out the door of the cottage. As he crossed the threshold, however, Maschler made one final pitch: "I think you could do something that no one has ever done before." Indeed, Williams would exceed Maschler's wildest expectations—and other's nightmares.

Thinking the meeting had not borne fruit, Maschler was surprised when Williams called him a few weeks later. The previously demure artist offered a rambling pitch about riddles and treasure. Maschler could barely follow, but he knew Williams' brainchild was special. Williams had grown frustrated by the way so-called readers leafed quickly through illustrated books. So, inspired by the Victorian puzzle books he pored over in his youth, Williams decided to craft an art book based around a puzzle, one that could not be solved using the book alone. Instead, this book would require readers to search the artwork for clues, and then employ clues in the real world. Thus, *Masquerade* was born. Although Williams didn't know it, the name of the book foreshadowed at least one impostor.

The story itself was straightforward enough: Jack Hare carries a treasure from the feminine Moon to the masculine Sun. He loses the treasure on the way, and readers are tasked with studying the book to find it. But the puzzle was as complicated as the story was simple. Indeed, the one person to whom Williams revealed the details had serious doubts that it could ever be solved. And they may have been right.

On August 7, 1979, more than three years after his initial meeting with Maschler, Williams set out to bury the golden hare pendant that he had crafted himself from precious metal and jewels. He was accompanied by Bamber Gascoigne, a respected television host recruited to serve as a celebrity witness. Graciously, Maschler had allowed Williams his independence as he crafted *Masquerade*. As Williams and Gascoigne drove to bury the pendant, Gascoigne began to wonder if that was a mistake. His fears were soon confirmed.

While others fretted over the potential difficulty of *Masquerade*, Williams was concerned that the solution might be too simple. After all, readers needed only to study 15 illustrations, draw a line from a depicted figure's left eye through the longest digits on its left hand and foot, then repeat the process with the right side, to reveal letters in the words surrounding each image, which—using other clues, including a reference to Sir Isaac Newton—could be arranged to read "Catherine's Long Finger Over Shadows Earth Buried Yellow Amulet Midday Points the Hour in Light of Equinox Look You." Far from too simple, Gascoine believed the solution was "infinitely more complex than Kit realized."

Once a treasure hunter had the proper words, a hidden acrostic—CLOSE BY AMPTHILL—would point them to Ampthill Park in

Bedfordshire, specifically to the park's cross-shaped monument to Catherine of Aragon. In a touch presaging *Raiders of the Lost Ark*, one would need to dig where the monument's shadow pointed at noon on the day of the equinox to unearth the pendant's ceramic casket, inscribed with the legend, "I am the keeper of the jewel of Masquerade, which lies waiting safe inside me for you or eternity." If Gascoine's suspicions were correct, it might be eternity.

Ignorant of Gascoine's concerns, Maschler was in overdrive with publicity, including full-color magazine spreads and a spot on BBC News. The initial print run of 60,000 copies sold out within days. By Christmas, *Masquerade* had knocked Frederick Forsyth's most recent thriller, *The Devil's Alternative*, to the no. 2 spot on the bestseller list. Maschler had been counting on the book to be a success, but neither he nor the book's mastermind had reckoned with the number of responses they would receive.

Maschler and Williams announced that it was not necessary to dig up the pendant to win. They would accept the first correctly worded answer mailed to them. Thousands of letters flooded John Cape's offices, some from as far away as Japan, Australia, and South Africa. Since no one at the publishing firm knew the answer, they were forwarded to Williams, who reviewed hundreds of responses each day. Between the letters and numerous interviews—and even a tour to America—Williams, who had hoped *Masquerade* would further his career as an artist, ironically found he had no time left for art.

So many people suspected that Williams had buried the pendant close to home that his neighbors began to tell strangers there was no Kit Williams living in Gloucestershire. Nearby Haresfield Beacon was dug up so many times that Williams was forced to pay for a sign telling treasure hunters they were digging in the wrong spot. One woman submitted every combination of latitude and longitude, sometimes sending dozens of letters a day. An American airline ran special flights, even giving traveling treasure hunters a commemorative shovel. *Masquerade* madness had hit. But for more than a year, no one came close to solving the puzzle.

Suspicions began to arise that maybe it was all a publicity stunt. Maschler convinced Williams to put together an additional clue that appeared in the *Sunday Times* the week before Christmas in 1980. The following year, a treasure hunter named Peter Ormandy came close to guessing the solution, even narrowing it down to Ampthill Park, but his reasoning was incorrect. Since he had corresponded with Williams, Williams panicked that his personal involvement might jeopardize the contest. While all this drama was occurring, two physics teachers were beginning their own hunt.

Mark Barker and John Rousseau spent part of New Year's Day, 1981, studying *Masquerade*, which Rousseau had originally purchased for his daughter. The pair approached the puzzle as scientists, gradually dissecting Williams' book—possibly the only people to do so without outside help. By the end of 1981, they had accurately predicted where to find the treasure, but rather than notifying Williams, they dug.

Initially planning to wait for the spring equinox in March of 1982, they instead used special equipment to predict where they should dig. But after two failed Early 1982, they decided to wait until the actual equinox. By then, however, it would be too late.

On February 19, 1982, the day after Barker and Rousseau's second attempted dig, Williams received a letter from Ken Thomas with a solution that was roughly accurate. Although it was clear that Thomas had not properly solved the puzzle, time and frustration had worn down Williams. He wanted it to be over. So, he called Thomas to tell him that he had deduced the correct location and he should go and dig. Surprisingly, Thomas was disinterested. He would dig another day, he said. It would only get stranger.

A few days later, Thomas called Williams again to report that he had recovered the hare pendant. Then he refused to answer calls for a week, and when he returned, he agreed to only two interviews—one for a newspaper, one for television. When his TV interview was conducted, he demanded his voice be distorted. And when there was a public unveiling of the pendant, he attended with a cap pulled over his face and his back to the cameras. The explanation for this strange behavior wouldn't come until years later, when it was revealed that Ken Thomas did not exist.

In the immediate aftermath, there was much dissatisfaction with the treasure hunt. Many treasure hunters refused to believe that Thomas had truly claimed the prize, while others spoke of a conspiracy between the artist and the publisher. But that didn't stop *Masquerade's* legacy.

Even before the treasure was discovered, there had been an Italian version. A decade later, a golden owl would be buried with similar clues in France, leading to a treasure hunt lasting over thirty years. In America, the hunt for Fenn's Fortune would be more dangerous, claiming at least five lives. But *Masquerade's* influence extended beyond the real world and into the digital.

Not long after the man claiming to be Ken Thomas claimed the prize, Great Britain, and the world, turned toward a new craze—computers. *Alkemstone*, a video game published in 1981, remains unsolved to this day. *Pimania*, from 1982, was solved three years later. Atari's *Swordquest* series was clearly influenced by *Masquerade*, and artist Roy Thomas said that Atari abandoned plans to bury that game's treasures after the issues with *Masquerade* became apparent. Many puzzle games today cross multiple media, an homage to the work pioneered by Williams. But the strangest game to be inspired by *Masquerade* would eventually lead to the truth behind Ken Thomas.

In 1984, a new software company called Haresoft offered a two-part game called *Hareraiser*. Almost like a digital version of *Masquerade*, *Hareraiser* required players (who had to purchase both parts) to explore various settings in an effort to gather clues. Decades later, comedian and computer game historian Stuart Ashen would describe it as "quite possibly the worst video game ever." In a bit of foreshadowing, the only good review came from a Mrs. Widdowson, who was later revealed to be working for the game's developers. Gameplay was nonsensical and there appeared to be no solution. But there was a prize offered: the very same hare pendant Ken Thomas had claimed.

Of course, no one ever solved *Hareraiser*. Haresoft went into liquidation and the pendant was sold at Sotheby's. Tom Maschler took the opportunity to publicize *Masquerade* once more, while Kit Williams tried to purchase his pendant back, but was outbid. The story caught the attention of newspaper editor Frank Branston, who had previously investigated a tale about a man who claimed to know where the pendant was buried long before the so-called "Ken Thomas" dug it up. Branston began his own treasure hunt of sorts.

The pieces fell into place fairly quickly. In December 1988, the truth of the so-called "Ken Thomas" was finally revealed in an article for *The Sunday Times*. Haresoft had been owned by two men, Dugald Thompson and John Guard. Guard's girlfriend, Veronica Robertson, had once dated Kit Williams with whom she had picnicked at Ampthill Park on the day he decided on the pendant's hiding place. Robertson shared this information with Guard. Knowing his indirect connection might come out quickly, Guard turned to his business partner, Dugald Thompson aka Ken Thomas.

Even today, some details remain unknown, such as the exact dynamic between Thompson and Guard, or why Thompson chose the name Ken Thomas. It is speculated that although Thompson and Guard knew to look in Ampthill Park, it wasn't until they saw the handiwork of physics teachers Barker and Rousseau that they knew exactly where. Indeed, it may be that Barker and Rousseau had actually unearthed the pendant, failed to see it in the dirt, and the opportunistic Thompson and Guard snatched it up. What is known, however, is that the pair used the prize as collateral to create Haresoft.

Although *The Sunday Times* article provided a degree of closure to what is likely the wildest treasure hunt in British history, it was a melancholy conclusion. Williams said, "This tarnishes *Masquerade* and I'm shocked by what has emerged. I feel a deep sense of responsibility to all those many people who were genuinely looking for it. Although I didn't know it, it was a skeleton in my cupboard and I'm relieved it has come out." But what of the precious hare pendant?

After its sale at auction in 1988, the jewel-encrusted rabbit disappeared for many years. Then, in July of 2009, the BBC produced a special on *Masquerade*. Williams, who had returned to painting, spoke about the hunt and the scandal for the first time in two decades, and expressed a desire to see the pendant again. The granddaughter of the current owner, an anonymous buyer in Asia, reunited Williams with the treasure he crafted. "I recognize my own work, I suppose in the way the mother would recognize her babies," Williams said upon handling the hare pendant for the first time in more than thirty years. "I made this thinking this is something really special…and it turned out that way."

## GAME OVER FOR ATARI "CHAMP"

On November 30, 2012, for the first time in its history, Guinness World Records created a new accolade. The world-renowned organization recognized veteran gamer Todd Rogers for holding the longest-standing video game high score. According to the newly created record, three decades earlier Rogers had achieved an unbeaten time of 5.51 seconds on the Atari 2600 game *Dragster*. There was just one problem: a time of 5.51 seconds was not possible.

Born on December 1, 1964, in Oaklawn, Illinois, Todd Rogers led a typical suburban childhood, his time divided between playing sports and collecting comic books. Then, in 1972, Rogers got his first taste for the medium that would change his life. At a mere eight years of age, an Odyssey system was made a staple in his living room. Rogers and his older brother spent hours besting one another at Pong and other rudimentary video games. Then, five years later, there was another world-changing milestone for the young video gamer. In 1977, a new console would usurp the Odyssey's role in the Rogers household: The Atari 2600. But the game that would forever change Rogers life was yet to be created by a company that didn't exist.

In 1980, Activision, a company created by disgruntled former employees of Atari, released *Dragster*, its first game for the popular console. An unlicensed port of the Kee-Games arcade coin-op *Drag Race*, it was programmed by Activision co-founder David Crane. In the game, the player races against the clock (or another player) to complete a ¼ mile track in the fastest time. As with Activision's other titles, a club was formed to recognize the most talented gamers. Those who reached the finish line in less than six seconds were invited to join Activision's official World Class Dragster Club.

On December 1, 1980, at age 16, Rogers proclivity for video games paid off. He became a certified member of the World Class Dragster Club with a time of 5.64 seconds. It was an honor that was memorialized by Activision on Official Membership Certificate no. 157. In the years that followed, Rogers continued to earn membership to Activision's various honorary game clubs. Then in 1982, Activision invited Rogers to demonstrate their games at Consumer Electronics Show, a role that would continue for the next few years. It was during this time that Rogers achieved another breakthrough. He had bested his previous *Dragster* high-score completing the game in a record-setting 5.51 seconds. Once again, the World Class Dragster Club recognized his achievement, this time, with a notice in the Spring 1983 edition of Activision's official newsletter.

In spite of his early success, Guinness did not recognize Rogers until 2012. It was at that time that a new honor was created among the annals of the world-record keepers. On November 30 of that year, Guinness acknowledged that Rogers had achieved a milestone unique even for the multiple-record holder. He had held an unbeaten high score for longer than any other gamer. But just six years later, Rogers' record would be wiped from the record books. And not because someone had fared better than Rogers' time of 5.51 seconds.

Instead, in 2017, just five years after he achieved a Guinness World Record, Rogers' score began to be challenged in a different manner. While the score had been suspected as impossible for years, an official dispute was opened with Twin Galaxies, the organization that has documented video game high scores for nearly 40 years. Included among the growing evidence of foul play, was the work of computer scientist Eric "Omnigamer" Koziel. After analyzing the *Dragster's* computer code, Omnigamer determined that the best possible time that could be achieved on the game is 5.57 seconds. To be sure, Twin Galaxies asked noted hacker and modder Ben Heck to work with Rogers to see if 5.51 could be reached. But even with Rogers' guidance, Heck was unable to replicate Rogers' alleged score of 5.51 seconds.

If *Dragster* couldn't be completed in 5.51 seconds, how did Rogers' score come to be acknowledged by the prestigious Guinness World Records? According to Guinness, they had relied on the records of Twin Galaxies. In turn, the original owner of Twin Galaxies, Walter Day, indicated that Twin Galaxies had relied upon Activision's certification. This was odd, however, because Twin Galaxies usually required a high score to be achieved live or for videotaped evidence to be submitted.

For their part, Activision had relied on a polaroid provided by a young Rogers in 1983. But Activision didn't require gamers to write their scores on the photographs submitted for admission to the World Class Dragster Club. So, many believe it's likely the photo was actually that of a 5.57 score that only appeared to be 5.51 due to screen glare or other issues that made the image difficult to read.

Even if a 5.51 had been achieved, however, Twin Galaxies reliance on Activision to determine the *Dragster* record holder is flawed. Because in the Spring 1983 issue of Activision's newsletter, the one that acknowledged Roger's score, two other gamers were noted to have achieved the same time of 5.51. In fact, according to an earlier edition of the publication, these two gamers had scored 5.51 a year earlier than Rogers. Further, the next best score according to Twin Galaxies was 5.64, which completely ignored the achievement of the other gamers.

It's not known who entered Rogers' score into the Twin Galaxies database in 2001. It's known, however, that Rogers was employed by Twin Galaxies from 1999 until 2012. And in 2013, Rogers admitted that he did enter his own scores on occasion.

Under scrutiny, Rogers' other unusual high scores on Twin Galaxies were questioned.

- The alleged video documenting Rogers' score of 15 million points on NES' port of *Donkey Kong* were discovered to be missing or non-existent.

- Rogers' time of 32.04 seconds in *Barnstorming* was discovered to be impossible to achieve even with all the obstacles removed from the game.
- Rogers' had a high score in *Wabbit* of 1,698 points even though the game ends when a player reaches 1,300 and the score only increases in increments of five points.
- It was confirmed that Rogers' score in *Fathom* would have taken 325 hours to achieve.
- Finally, Rogers' alleged score of 65 million points on Atari 5200's *Centipede* far exceeded the second-place record holder of 58,078 points.

On January 29, 2018, faced with a growing number of complaints that Rogers had falsified his time, and the increasing pile of evidence suggesting his 5.51-second run on *Dragster* was impossible, Twin Galaxies threw out all of Rogers's records and banned him for life from its scoreboards. And following that disqualification from the Twin Galaxies scoreboard, Guinness World Records removed Rogers' record for the longest-standing video game high score.

While Rogers' dubious notoriety far outlasted his fraudulent *Dragster* time, it seems it was Rogers that helped speed his fame to an end. It was only shortly after Rogers was acknowledged by Guinness that his *Dragster* and other scores began to be scrutinized. In a curious bit of karma, the reason Guinness had created a new record for Rogers, more than three decades after his alleged achievement, is because Rogers himself had lobbied the organization for four years to do so.

## THE MYSTERY OF THE GARFIELD PHONE

The Garfield phone was advertised in the 1980s as a "real phone for real fun." It featured a keypad, had a classic electric ring—and the cartoon cat's eyelids slid half-open when the user picked up the handset. But in a world once dominated by the dull Princess phone, how did the novelty communication device come to be? And more importantly, how did it come to stand for environmental disaster?

It was around 1984. Fueled by tax cuts and interest adjustments, the United States continued to climb out of the recession that plagued the decade. Stock prices were on the rise, and so was consumer spending. But it was America's obsession with a particular cartoon cat that could not be contained. Literally. For one of the most popular objects of American consumerism appeared on a distant shore in a most unusual way.

Rene Morvan was 19 years old, living on the coast of Brittany, France. Except for the occasional storm, it was an otherwise quiet farming community. On a fateful day in 1984, a particularly nasty weather phenomenon lured Morvan to the idyllic shores of Brittany. There, he noticed something unusual. Sure, the violent waters were known to deposit all matter of sea life on the coast. But the orange debris on the French beach, which was strewn here and there, was too brightly colored to be natural.

Upon inspection, Morvan learned that the unusual refuse was chunks of plastic—the first pieces of a larger puzzle. And as each successive wave delivered another batch, Morvan followed a trail being revealed before him. Finally, venturing down the rocky cliffside, Morvan discovered the source of the waste. But he would keep it a secret for thirty-five years.

Founded in 1926, the legendary toy manufacturer Tyco had weathered The Great Depression by aiding the military during World War II. And by the 1970s, Tyco had become the leading manufacturer of HO-scale trains. At that time, however, Tyco's earnings began to go off the rails. To place the company back on track, a new management team sought licensing agreements with brands that would expand the toy company's offerings and bottom line. And while they would later be known for a certain ticklish puppet, it was one particular license that birthed a Tyco product that would survive long after the brand was defunct.

Born in 1945, Jim Davis wanted to be a farmer like his father. His asthma, however, had other plans for him. Often forced to remain indoors, Davis discovered his love of drawing. But it wasn't until 1978, when he finally created a hit. It was then that Garfield, his cynical comic tabby, with a penchant for lasagna and a hatred for Mondays, had been syndicated in 41 newspapers. This success bred a litter of other opportunities. And in 1981, just a few years after licensing fees had made George Lucas extremely wealthy, Davis created Paws, Inc., a company to manage the Garfield brand. And soon, many Garfield-related products flooded the market. But only one of those also flooded the coastline of Brittany, France.

In 1982, a consent decree, agreed to by AT&T and the U.S. government, ended the telephone monopoly the company had held for decades. Just five years earlier, a court ruling allowed competing manufacturers to offer designer telephones that would add a unique style to consumer's homes. Suddenly, the phone was no longer a standardized, leased portal into AT&T's network. Alexander Graham Bell's invention now came in an assortment of novel forms that included Coca-Cola bottles, peekaboo Lucite globes and by 1981 one popular, albeit cantankerous, orange tabby cat.

Not long after Rene Morvan first discovered bits of orange plastic washing up on the beach of quaint Brittany, France, others also took notice. It was impossible not to. Shortly after the storm that first delivered the unusual flotsam to the shore in 1984, more debris followed. This time, the pieces were complete enough to recognize the culprit: hundreds of early-1980s Garfield phones. And while clean-up efforts immediately followed, their task was Sisyphean. For as soon as the novelty devices were cleared from the beaches, the next tide would deposit another batch, the smug expression of the faux feline mocking its would-be captors.

Clean-up efforts continued for decades. And while it was long suspected that an errant shipping container was the source, none could be found. Led by Claire Simonin-Le Meur, president of the environmental group Ar Viltansou, volunteers renewed cleaning efforts in 2018. Out of concern for the environment, Simonin-Le Meur had been searching for the origin of Garfield for years. Believing the source of the cargo to be under the sea, the environmentalists enlisted the help of divers and submarines. Unfortunately, none spotted anything below the waters, and fewer believed a container could be there. Paws, Inc., the company that currently licenses Garfield, couldn't verify the decades-old tale of the wayward shipping boat. But a fateful meeting on the beach in 2019 changed everything.

"Are you looking for Garfield?" the middle-aged man asked Simonin-Le Meur, as she continued her clean-up efforts on the Brittany coastline. When Simonin-Le Meur affirmed the man's inquiry, the man continued. "Come with me." Now in his mid-fifties, Rene Morvan explained how 35 years earlier, at 19 years of age, he had observed the orange phones dotting the beach after a storm. As he detailed his descent down the rocky cliffs into a sea cave, he led Simonin-Le Meur to the site of his discovery. Tucked deep within the recesses of the Earth, he assured her, he had found a metal shipping container, stuffed with the feline phones. But when they reached the supposed location of the find, another problem became obvious: the cave had vanished!

As fate would have it, for most of the year, the cave is rendered inaccessible by the tide. Fortunately, just a few weeks after Morvan came forward, the entrance to the underwater cavern revealed itself. As volunteers scaled the cliffs to the entrance of the cave, they stumbled upon bits of Garfield scattered across the rocks. Their hope was to find the lost shipping container still brimming with phones. In that way, they could stop more debris from polluting their ocean. But their hopes—unlike the plastic phones, which still remain largely intact—were soon dashed. For what they found was the remainder of the shipping container. And it was empty.

While environmentalists have resolved the mystery of the Garfield phones, they did not celebrate their discovery. With the bulk of the phones already gone, "the sea," said Simonin-Le Meur, "has done its job for 30 years. We arrived after the battle." For many, the face of the lasagna-loving cat brings a nostalgic joy fueled by its surging popularity in the 1980s. For others, it's the comic poster child for pollution and long-lasting environmental damage wrought by plastics. Per Simonin-Le Meur, there is "a feeling of desolation and sadness." Or as Garfield might put it: "Mondays."

## ABOUT THE AUTHOR

Growing up a latchkey in the 1980s, in the heart of Jersey City, NJ, Will Padilla was raised by pop culture. He-Man made Will believe he had the power. And Spielberg encouraged him to seek adventure. So, in his youth Will's Huffy became an X-Wing and the abandoned factory on his city block became the Death Star. And as his own 1980 coming-of-age story entered its denouement, Will's love of media had him longing to entertain.

First pursuing acting, Will trained at The Shakespeare Theatre of New Jersey (as a company member alongside Peter Dinklage, future star of *Game of Thrones*), at Bill Esper Studios (New York) and with Olympia Dukakis. Will performed in productions throughout New York and New Jersey, including those at the Shakespeare Theatre of New Jersey and Paper Mill Playhouse. Additionally, Will appeared in fledgling plays at Columbia University, The Collective (Williamstown Theatre Festival), Playwrights Theatre of New Jersey, and Ensemble Studio Theatre.

Frustrated with the audition process, Will next turned to writing. He adapted John Milton's epic poem *Paradise Lost* into a dark commedia, which was produced at HERE (New York) as part of the American Living Room Festival. Will also wrote and performed with Those Lazy

Bastards (New York) a sketch comedy group that he founded with (now legendary voice actor) Yuri Lowenthal.

Having consumed hours of Harold Faltermeyer, and having studied music theory at university, Will additionally composed and designed sound for theater. He scored *Goodbye, My Friduchita* (starring Tony Award winner Priscilla Lopez) at The Director's Company (New York), then transferred to Off-Broadway; *The Duchess of Malfi* (directed by Michael Kahn), *Mojo* (starring Glen Howerton of *It's Always Sunny in Philadelphia*), *Pains of Youth* and *Macbeth*, all at The Juilliard School (New York); and *Romeo and Juliet* (directed by Erica Schmidt future screenwriter of *Cyrano*) at Present Company Theatorium (New York).

Since 2019, Will has been hosting *1980s Now*. Joined by his co-hosts, Kat and Jon, the weekly podcast demonstrates that nostalgia alone doesn't account for the contemporary fascination with their favorite decade. Instead, they share personal experiences and interview experts to demonstrate how the "era of greed" bore the greatest moments in movies, music and television—and that those continue to influence media today. 1980s Now has covered a wide variety of topics, including punk rock, movie stunts, and classic video games. To date, Will has spoken with countless 1980s icons like Ernie Hudson, Taylor Dayne, Cassandra Peterson, Dee Wallace and Sir Mix-A-Lot.

In addition to this book, Will has just completed *Outcastes*, a novel set in the 1980s that follows a group of misfit teens coming-of-age during the nascent era of hip hop culture. Will's work will also soon be featured in the upcoming collection of essays on 1980s music *Life Goes On: The*

*Lessons We Learned from 1980s Music*. Visit 1980snow.com for more information.

## ACKNOWLEDGEMENTS

Thanks to Kat O'Connor and Jon Reddick, my co-hosts on the *1980s Now* podcast. Their curiosity, humor, and support have kept me motivated to research and write these tales.

Thanks to L. Ray Sexton, the co-creator and original co-host of *1980s Now*. Without him, we wouldn't have had an initial home for these unbelievable stories.

Thanks to George W. Krubski and Marcus Taylor for their contributions to this book and the *1980s Now* podcast. Their work has elevated both endeavors.

Finally, thanks to the many patrons who have supported *1980s Now* over the years. You've not only helped fund the production of the show, but you've fueled our spirits. A special thanks to the following, who were patrons as of this writing: Craig Anderson, Matt Blocker, Brad Bowman, Tony Grate, Brandon Greer, Nich Guillory, John Henderson, Matt Marino, Kyle Paladino, @retrodolls77, Rick Parker, Keith Sheehan, Marcus Taylor, Nate Wallace, and Lucy Webb.

# SOURCES

### Strangest Things: The Montauk Project

Felton, J. (2023, May 24). *The Real Story Behind The Infamous "Philadelphia Experiment"*. IFL Science. https://www.iflscience.com/the-real-story-behind-the-infamous-philadelphia-experiment-69075

Nichols, P. B., & Moon, P. (1992). *The Montauk Project: Experiments in Time*. Sky Books.

### The Adventure for Swordquest

Grundhauser, E. (2016, March 8). *The Quest for the Real-Life Treasures of Atari's Swordquest*. Atlas Obscura. https://www.atlasobscura.com/articles/the-quest-for-the-reallife-treasures-of-ataris-swordquest

Hardie, J. (1998). *Michael S. Rideout*. Atari Compendium. https://www.ataricompendium.com/archives/interviews/michael_rideout/interview_michael_rideout.html

*InformationSwordQuestEarthWorld*. (n.d.). Atari Mania. https://www.atarimania.com/game-atari-2600-vcs-swordquest-earthworld_25679.html

JacobZu7zu7. (2006, August 10). *Swordquest Earthworld = Bad or Good?* AtariAge. https://forums.atariage.com/topic/91883-swordquest-earthworld-bad-or-good/page/2/

McWhertor, M. (2017, February 20). *Atari's bringing back its Swordquest comics*. Polygon. https://www.polygon.com/2017/2/20/14678122/atari-swordquest-comics-return-dynamite-entertainment

*ScreenshotsSwordQuestFireWorld*. (n.d.). Atari Mania. https://www.atarimania.com/game-atari-2600-vcs-swordquest-fireworld_25680.html

Stilphen, S. (n.d.). *John-Michael Battaglia*. Digit Press. https://www.digitpress.com/library/interviews/interview_john-michael_battaglia.html

Stilphen, S. (2025, February 22). *SwordQuest Revisited*. Atari Compendium. https://www.ataricompendium.com/archives/articles/swordquest_revisited/swordquest_revisited.html

Webster, A. (2022, November 11). *Atari 50 is an incredible playable tour through video game history*. The Verge. https://www.theverge.com/23451349/atari-50-review-xbox-playstation-switch-steam

## The Most Artful Museum Heist

Branigin, W. (1989, July 31). ROBBERY, RECOVERY AND RELIEF BEHIND MEXICO'S ARCHAEOLOGICAL NEAR-CATASTROPHE. *The Washington Post*.

Morales Olea, D. (2024, September 22). *The robbery of the century: How two students stole 124 pieces from an iconic Mexican museum in 1985*. El País. https://english.elpais.com/culture/2024-09-22/the-robbery-of-the-century-how-two-students-stole-124-pieces-from-an-iconic-mexican-museum-in-1985.html

## The Real Cocaine Bear

Denton, S. (2016). *The Bluegrass Conspiracy: An Inside Story of Power, Greed, Drugs & Murder*. CreateSpace Independent Publishing Platform.

Mendoza, J. (2022, November 29). *The Wild Life Of Cop-Turned-Criminal Andrew Thornton, The Man Behind Kentucky's Cocaine Bear*. The Grunge. https://www.grunge.com/1119185/the-wild-life-of-cop-turned-criminal-andrew-thornton-the-man-behind-kentuckys-cocaine-bear/

## 1999: The Accidental Prophecy

Brady, F. (1989). *Citizen Welles: A Biography of Orson Welles*. University Press of Kentucky.

Callow, S. (2006). *Orson Welles: Hello Americans*. Viking.

Callow, S. (2015). *Orson Welles: One-Man Band*. Viking.

Callow, S. (1995). *Orson Welles: The Road to Xanadu*. Viking.

Carringer, R. (1996). *The Making of Citizen Kane*. University of California Press.

Goldfarb, A. (2021, February 17). *How Orson Welles Became the Most Infamous Pitchman in Booze History*. InsideHook. https://www.insidehook.com/article/food-and-drink/most-infamous-pitchman-orson-welles

Greenman, B. (2017). *Dig If You Will the Picture: Funk, Sex, God and Genius in the Music of Prince*. St. Martin's Press.

Guenette, R. (Director). (1981). *The Man Who Saw Tomorrow* [Film]. Filmways Pictures.

Hahn, A. (2003). *Possessed: The Rise and Fall of Prince*. Billboard Books.

Heylin, C. (2005). *Despite the System: Orson Welles Versus the Hollywood Studios*. Chicago Review Press.

Husney, O. (2018). *Famous People Who've Met Me: A Memoir by the Man Who Discovered Prince*. Plane Reader Publishing.

Jones, C. (1975). *Rikki-Tikki-Tavi* [TV movie]. CBS.

Jones, J. (9 Oct. 2015). Orson Welles and the Art of Selling Out. *The Guardian*.

Leaming, B. (1985). *Orson Welles: A Biography*. Viking.

Light, A. (2014). *Let's Go Crazy: Prince and the Making of Purple Rain*. Atria Books.

McBride, J. (2006). *Whatever Happened to Orson Welles?: A Portrait of an Independent Career*. University Press of Kentucky.

Parsons. A. (1976). *The Alan Parsons Project: Tales of Mystery and Imagination* [Album]. 20th Century Records.

Prince. (Director). (1987). *Sign o' the Times* [Film]. Paisley Park Films.

Ro, R. (2011). *Prince: Inside the Music and the Masks*. St. Martin's Press.

Rosen, M. (Director). (1978). *Watership Down* [Film]. Nepenthe Productions.

Schwartz, A. (2015). *Broadcast Hysteria: Orson Welles's War of the Worlds and the Art of Fake News*. Hill and Wang.

Shin, N. (Director). (1983). *Transformers: The Movie* [Film]. Hasbro.

Thompson, F. (1996). *Lost Films: Important Movies That Disappeared*. Citadel.

Tucker, K. (1981). Prince's Ill-Fated Opening Act for the Stones. *Los Angeles Herald-Examiner*.

Welles, O. (30 Oct. 1938). *The War of the Worlds. The Mercury Theatre on the Air* [Radio broadcast]. CBS Radio.

Whitburn, J. (2004). *Top R&B/Hip-Hop Singles: 1942–2004*. Record Research.

## The Rendlesham Incident

Butler, B., & Randles, J. (1984). *Sky Crash: A Cosmic Conspiracy*. Neville Spearman.

Kinsella, P., & Butler, B. (2022). *SKY CRASH THROUGHOUT TIME: UFOs, The Reptilian Man & Strange Mysteries Surrounding Rendlesham*. Independently Published.

Ridpath, I. (2025). *The Rendlesham Forest UFO Case*. http://www.ianridpath.com/ufo/rendlesham.html

Rigby, N. (2020, December 26). *Rendlesham Forest UFO: Are we any closer to the truth 40 years on?* BBC. https://www.bbc.com/news/uk-england-suffolk-54649675

## Rapper's Delight: These Are the Good Crimes

Beal, D. (2012, July 1). *Jody Williams on His Return*. Believer Magazine. https://www.thebeliever.net/jody-williams-on-his-return/

Bellware, K. (2023, August 15). The unlikely origins of 'Rapper's Delight,' hip-hop's first mainstream hit. *The Washington Post*.

Charnas, D. (2023, February 7). *The Rise and Fall of Hip-Hop's First Godmother: Sugar Hill Records' Sylvia Robinson*. Billboard. https://www.billboard.com/music/rb-hip-hop/sugar-hill-records-sylvia-robinson-hip-hop-godmother-8533108/

Edgers, G. (2016, September 29). They took Grandmaster Caz's rhymes without giving him credit. Now, he's getting revenge. *The Washington Post*.

Johnson, K. (2015, February 26). *Truth Be Told: An interview with Chip Shearin*. No Treble. https://www.notreble.com

Murphy, K. (2023, August 11). *How Sugar Hill Records remade music with "Rapper's Delight"*. Los Angeles Times. https://www.latimes.com/entertainment-arts/music/story/2023-08-07/sugar-hill-records-gang-sylvia-robinson-rappers-delight-1979-50th-anniversary-hip-hop

VladTV. (2014). *Grandmaster Caz Talks Big Bank Hank Stealing "Rapper's Delight"* [Video]. YouTube. https://www.youtube.com/watch?v=3FBXRUWraKo

**The Monster with 21 Faces**

Giacomazzo, B. (2021, December 27). *How 'The Monster With 21 Faces' Terrorized Japan During The Harrowing Glico Morinaga Incident*. All That's Interesting. https://allthatsinteresting.com/monster-with-21-faces

Peters, L. (2019, August 12). *Unresolved: The Monster With 21 Faces, The Glico-Morinaga Case, And The Candy Poisoning Incident Of 1984*. The Ghost in My Machine. https://theghostinmymachine.com/2019/08/12/unresolved-the-monster-with-21-faces-the-glico-morinaga-case-and-the-candy-poisoning-incident-of-1984-kidnapping-katsuhisa-ezaki-extortion-unsolved-fox-eyed-man-video-man/

Whelan, M. (2019, June 2). *The Monster With 21 Faces*. Unresolved. https://unresolved.me/the-monster-with-21-faces

**The Cabbage Patch Paternity Suit**

Associated Press. (1986, August 30). Judge Agrees to Put Lid on Garbage Pail Kids. *Los Angeles Times*.

*BabyLand General Hospital*. (n.d.) Roadside America. https://www.roadsideamerica.com/story/2074

Booth Conroy, S. (1983, November 29). Soft Dolls, Hard Cash. *The Washington Post*.

Brozyna, E. (2022, July 19). *What Happened to Cabbage Patch Kids, the Dolls That Caused a Huge Frenzy in the '80s?* PureWow. https://www.purewow.com/entertainment/what-happened-to-cabbage-patch-kids

Denson, B. (2021, December 1). *Cabbage Patch Crazy: The First Holiday Toy to Bring Us to Blows Was a Court Fight Too*. Medium. https://medium.com/smorgasbord-of-history/cabbage-patch-crazy-the-first-holiday-toy-to-bring-us-to-blows-was-a-court-fight-too-e0c85a09042d

Jedeikin, D. (2021). *The Insane True Story of the Cabbage Patch Doll Riots*. Mel Magazine. https://melmagazine.com/en-us/story/the-insane-true-story-of-the-cabbage-patch-doll-riots

Joyce, F. S. (1983, December 6). CABBAGE PATCH KIDS SPUR A BATTLE OVER PARENTAGE. *The New York Times*.

Lewis, E. (2021, November 22). *Look Back: Cabbage Patch stampede hit WB in 1983*. Times Leader. https://www.timesleader.com/news/1525251/look-back-cabbage-patch-stampede-hit-wb-in-1983

Lindenfeld Hall, S. (2016, December 1). *Scarce Toys: Cabbage Patch Kid theft, other stories of hard-to-find toys*. WRAL News. https://www.wral.com/story/scarce-toys-the-day-a-woman-ripped-a-doll-from-my-nine-year-old-hands/16288463/

Press, R. M. (1983, December 12). 'Custody' fight over Cabbage Patch dolls. *The Christian Science Monitor*.

Turner, C. (2022). *THE STORY OF: The Cabbage Patch Kids Dolls*. 29Secrets. https://29secrets.com/pop-culture/the-story-of-the-cabbage-patch-kids-dolls/

**Game Over for Atari "Champ"**

Alexandra, H. (2018, January 30). *Guinness officially nixes Todd Rogers' Dragster records*. Kotaku. https://kotaku.com/guinness-officially-nixes-todd-rogers-dragster-records-1822568394

Frank, A. (2018, January 31). *Longest-standing video game record declared 'impossible,' thrown out after 35 years*. Polygon. https://www.polygon.com/2018/1/29/16944736/atari-dragster-game-world-record-banned

Jobst, K. (2019, October 13). *The longest con in video game history* [Video file]. https://www.youtube.com/watch?v=PrH7aPmO61w

Moultrie, T. (2013, January 5). *INTERVIEW: Video game legend Todd Rogers talks about being the first pro gamer ever*. Complex. https://www.complex.com/pop-culture/2013/01/interview-video-game-legend-todd-rogers-talks-about-being-the-first-pro-gamer-ever

Rougeau, M. (2012, December 31). *The Longest-Standing Video Game World Record is Over 30 Years Old*. Complex. https://www.complex.com/pop-culture/2012/12/the-longest-standing-video-game-world-record-is-over-30-years-old

*Todd Rogers: The Man Behind the Legen.* (2001, January 24). Beat the Champ. http://beatthechamp.com/

Wang, A. B. (2021, November 27). *A man accused of cheating at video games may lose his Guinness World Record.* The Washington Post. https://www.washingtonpost.com/news/early-lead/wp/2018/01/29/a-man-accused-of-cheating-at-video-games-may-lose-his-decades-old-guinness-world-record/

## Masquerade

*Kit Williams's Golden Hare.* (2016, May 20). Filfire. https://www.filfre.net/2016/05/kit-williamss-golden-hare-part-1-the-contest/

*Kit Williams - 'The man behind the masquerade.'* (2009, December 1). BBC. http://news.bbc.co.uk/local/gloucestershire/hi/people_and_places/arts_and_culture/newsid_8388000/8388741.stm

*Masquerade and the mysteries of Kit Williams.* (n.d.). BunnyEars. https://bunnyears.net/kitwilliams/

Shields, M. (2019, April 5). *Masquerade: How a real-life treasure hunt obsessed a nation.* BBC. https://www.bbc.com/news/uk-england-beds-bucks-herts-47671776

## The Mystery of the Garfield Phone

Breakup of the Bell System. (2025, March 13). In Wikipedia. https://en.wikipedia.org/wiki/Breakup_of_the_Bell_System

*Garfield phones beach mystery finally solved after 35 years.* (2019, March 28). BBC. https://www.bbc.com/news/world-europe-47732553

Jim Davis (cartoonist). (2025, April 5). In Wikipedia. https://en.wikipedia.org/wiki/Jim_Davis_(cartoonist)

Karasz, P. (2019, March 29). *Why Do Garfield Phones Keep Washing Up on This Beach?* The New York Times. https://www.nytimes.com/2019/03/29/world/europe/garfield-phones-france.html

Heller, S. (2019, March 29). *Garfield phones have mysteriously washed up on a French beach for 30 years: 'It never stops'*. Business Insider. https://www.insider.com/mystery-garfield-phones-french-beach-solved-2019-3

Katz, B. (2019, April 1). *Washing Ashore in France for 30 Years?* Smithsonian Magazine. https://www.smithsonianmag.com/smart-news/why-have-garfield-phones-been-washing-ashore-france-30-years-180971835/

Vanderbilt, T. (2012, May 15). *Hello? A visual history of the telephone.* Slate. https://www.slate.com/articles/life/design/2012/05/telephone_design_a_brief_history_ photos_.html

www.ingramcontent.com/pod-product-compliance
Lightning Source LLC
Chambersburg PA
CBHW070634030426
42337CB00020B/4009